SLÖJD

The Swedish art of wood and textile handicrafts

KERSTIN
NEUMÜLLER

Photography by Ellinor Hall

BATSFORD

Foreword

The Swedish word slöjd derives from *slög,* an old expression used to describe a person who is clever, practical and skilled in handicrafts

Today, if you say the word to a Swedish person, *slöjd* will usually bring back memories of taking craft lessons at primary school, although the term means much more than that. To me, the concept is about using what you have to hand to make the things you want. In a wider sense, *slöjd* is a mentality that offers you the option to solve a problem without paying someone else to do it. I believe that by learning how to make the things you want you can build your confidence, increase your resilience, and create a mindset where you can start seeing solutions to any problem you might encounter in life.

This is a book for people who say, 'oh, I wish I could...'. It contains a range of craft projects that are suitable to make at home. Many of the projects take a 'use what you have' attitude to reusing materials, which I think makes crafting a bit more accessible for those trying something out for the first time.

My best tip for anyone who wants to learn a new craft is to prepare to fail a few times before you get the hang of it. I have implemented this tip so many times that I now get surprised if I succeed at something the first time I try it! It will certainly take longer for you to finish if you fail a few times along the way, and you may need more supplies, but if you allow yourself to let go of your inner perfectionist for a while, you will master the technique much better than if you didn't dare to make a 'mistake'.

Before you start, I would like to point out that it's only you who can judge whether something turned out well or not. If you think it's pretty, then it's pretty. Do these colours go well together? You decide. How something 'should' be isn't really that important! The only thing you really need to keep in mind is whether the object is fit for purpose: a potholder that is so thin you burn your fingers is not a good potholder, objectively speaking, but perhaps it could make a good dishcloth.

PS: I have written from a right-handed perspective – apologies to all left-handed readers.

Crochet a potholder

Crocheting a potholder is a good introductory project for those who are curious about crochet. I made mine from a thick weaving yarn and jute twine from a garden centre!

YOU WILL NEED
- Crochet hook
- Yarn
- Scissors
- Wool needle

Choosing your crochet hook and yarn

Crochet hooks come in many different sizes, and you usually choose the size according to the thickness of the yarn you're crocheting with.

There probably isn't any type of yarn that you can't use for crocheting. Anything from sewing thread and single-ply linen yarn to rags and rope can be crocheted, as long as you have a crochet hook that is up to the job!

I like to visit flea markets to look for yarns with nice colours. If it feels too thin when I start crocheting, I use two strands of the same yarn to crochet with to achieve the necessary thickness. A word of warning, however: when crocheting potholders, it can be best to stick to yarns made from plant fibres, such as linen, cotton, hemp or jute. Wool shrinks in the wash, while synthetic fibres such as polyester and acrylic run a risk of melting when they come into contact with heat.

How do I know if my crochet hook is too big?

The size of the stitches depends to a certain extent on how large the tip of the crochet hook is: if the tip is large, the stitches will also be large. If you think your crochet stitches are too loose, try using a smaller crochet hook.

How do I know if my crochet hook is too small?

What usually makes me swap to a larger crochet hook is if I can't pick up the whole yarn when picking up a new stitch. Sometimes, you only manage to catch half the yarn, which can be frustrating.

As with all tools, it's easy to have favourites. To be honest, I only have one metal crochet hook that I use regularly. It works for almost all yarns. When I was crocheting the potholders made from jute twine, I needed a larger hook, however, so I took out my knife and carved myself one. If you live close to a craft shop or flea market, it may of course be more convenient to run out and buy one.

1   2   3

Start crocheting

The most basic version of crocheting consists of two types of stitches: chain stitches and double crochet stitches (note that 'double crochet' is the UK term; the US term is 'single crochet'). Double crochet stitches are worked on top of a previous row of stitches, while chain stitches are stitches that are not fixed onto other stitches: they hang freely in a chain. To start your project, you first need to work a foundation chain of chain stitches that will become your starting point for the rest of the work.

Crochet chain stitches

Hold the yarn in your left hand and the crochet hook in your right hand. You will hold the work with your left-hand thumb and middle finger, while the index finger controls the tension of the yarn.

Twist the yarn around the crochet hook a few times, with the tail end hanging freely downwards. Try to hold the yarn as I do above. [1]

Catch the yarn with the crochet hook and pull a loop downwards, so that the yarn that was around the crochet hook's shaft slides over its tip. The yarn you have just hooked onto will follow through downwards and will form a new loop on the crochet hook's shaft. [2, 3] The new loop is your first chain stitch.

Now you can crochet a chain of chain stitches by repeating what you just did: catch the yarn with the crochet hook and pull it down through the loop on the crochet hook's shaft. When you make this movement, the loop that was around the crochet hook's shaft will slide over the crochet hook's tip,

4

5

and the yarn you pulled down with you forms a new loop around the crochet hook's shaft. Wrapping the yarn around the tip of the crochet hook, ready to be pulled through one or several loops, is called making a yarn over. [4] Decide how wide you want the potholder to be and make your foundation chain that size. You may want to add a couple of extra stitches because the work may pull together a bit as you work. Add one more chain: this is called the turning chain and accommodates the height of the next row. Now we will start the second row of our crochet work; for this, we will work in double crochet. This is similar to a chain stitch, but involves a few extra steps.

Row number 2: Double crochet

The first stitch of the next row is worked into the second chain from the hook. Look at the chain of chain stitches. On one of the sides the yarn sits in pairs: underneath them is where you insert the tip of your crochet hook. If you have done this correctly, you should end up in the middle of the chain, so you have two bars of yarn over the crochet hook and one under it. [5]

Make a yarn over and then pull the crochet hook out of the foundation chain. Now you have two loops on the crochet hook. [6]

6   7

Make another yarn over, and pull the crochet hook through both new loops. [7] Now you have only one loop on the hook again, and you have just made a double crochet stitch. Continue working double crochet stitches along the full length of the foundation chain. When you come to the end, make a chain stitch (turning chain) before you turn the work. What was the back of the work becomes the front of the work, and then you work another row of double crochet. Work your way back and forth along the potholder, from one side to the other and back again – always making one chain stitch before you start a new row.

Crochet doesn't have to be any more complicated than this. It's also super easy to unravel the work. Perhaps you accidentally skipped a few stitches, or want to start over to make the potholder a bit wider? Just take out the crochet hook and pull the yarn, and the stitches will start to unravel. When you think your potholder is the right size you can make a final chain stitch, cut the yarn 10–15cm (4–6in) away from the work and pull the end through the final stitch. When you pull the end of the yarn, the final stitch will close around it; this way the end is locked into place so the stitch can't unravel.

If you want to crochet a small loop to hang up the potholder, you can make a length of chain stitches secured into place with a double crochet stitch, then cut the yarn and pull the end through the last stitch.

Crochet a potholder

Changing colour

You can change colour when a row is completed by cutting the yarn and pulling it through the last chain stitch, then just start crocheting with a new colour. You can also change colour in the middle of a row if you want. Just cut the old end, leave it hanging at the back of the work, and start crocheting with the new colour. Leave the tail end hanging at the back of the work as well. When you have finished your potholder, you can secure all threads with a darning needle by sewing them into the back of the work with a few stitches.

Crochet in the round

To crochet a circular shape I start with a chain of five chain stitches, then I join them with a double crochet stitch. Then I crochet around the little ring I've made. Instead of inserting the crochet hook into the chain stitches, I insert it in the hole at the centre of the ring; this way, a little round hole is formed in the middle of the potholder, which I like.

Here, I crocheted eight stitches into this first round.

For the second round you will work in double crochet, but you will need to increase the number of stitches for each round to make sure the potholder remains flat rather than becoming bowl-shaped. You increase the number of stitches by making two stitches in the same stitch.

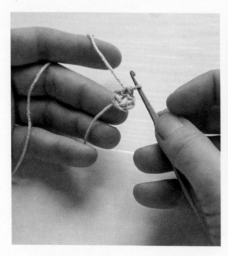 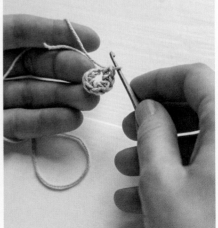

ROUND TWO Increase in every stitch.

ROUND THREE Increase in every other stitch, with a standard stitch in between.

ROUND FOUR Increase in every third stitch, with two standard stitches in between.

ROUND FIVE Increase in every fourth stitch, with three standard stitches in between.

Then I changed colour and continued working around and around. Every time I started a new round, I increased the number of standard double crochet stitches in between the increases by one. After a while it's difficult to see where the new round begins and the old one ends, so it's a good idea to mark the last stitch in a round with a safety pin or similar stitch marker. Insert the pin through the yarn of the stitch when you have worked it, then you know you have made one round when you come to it the next time.

Crochet a potholder

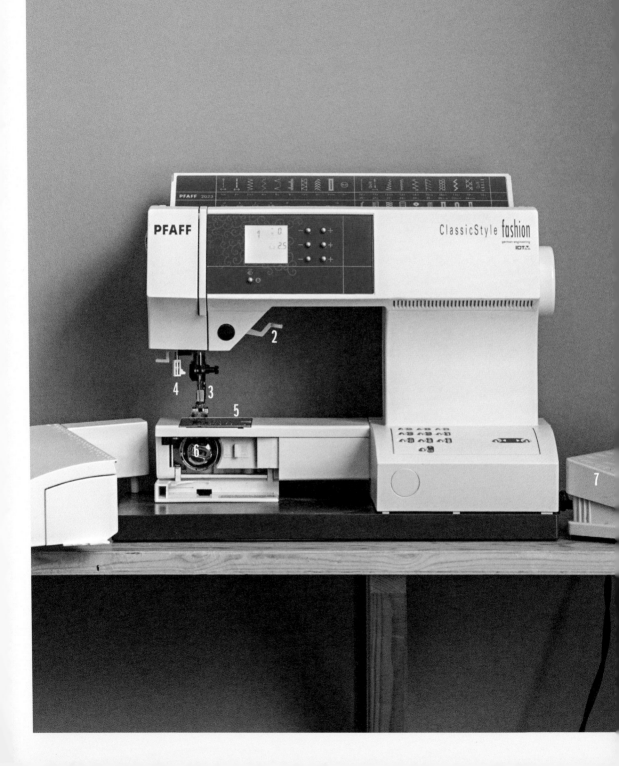

Sewing machines

Sewing machines can look a bit different depending on the model, but most work in a similar way.

1. A SPOOL of sewing thread is fitted at the top of the sewing machine. The thread runs from here down to the needle. This thread is called the TOP THREAD.
2. The presser foot is lifted up and down with a LEVER that is usually positioned at the back of the sewing machine.
3. The PRESSER FOOT keeps the fabric in place while you're sewing. It can be changed and comes in many different varieties, but I use the same one for almost everything I make.
4. The sewing machine's NEEDLE is held in place with a small screw that you need to loosen to be able to change it. Needles come in different thicknesses. As a general rule, the thicker your fabric, the thicker the needle required.
5. The THROAT PLATE on my sewing machine is made from metal, but some are made from plastic. This stops the needle from pushing the fabric down to the bottom thread bobbin.
6. The BOTTOM THREAD is inserted in the BOBBIN CASE. This small bobbin with its thread creates a seam together with the top thread. The bobbin is usually placed in its case so that the bobbin rotates clockwise. Before you can start sewing, the bottom thread needs to be fished out so that it comes out over the throat plate. The easiest way to do this is by threading the top thread in place in the machine and then sewing one stitch. The needle comes down through the throat plate; when it comes back up, it brings the end of the bottom thread with it.
7. The FOOT PEDAL is the sewing machine's 'accelerator': when you push it down, the machine will start sewing. There is no brake pedal, however!

Sewing

Sometimes it feels like it's more common for a sewing machine to be gathering dust in a cupboard because of some 'unknown fault' than actually being used. I know how frustrating it can be when the machine doesn't work and you just need to sew something quickly, but that's no excuse to banish it forever. It's absolutely worth getting it serviced to get it running again, but before you do, there are a few things you can try to get your machine in order:

CHECK THE THREAD TENSION

All sewing machines come with a manual. If you have lost yours, you can probably find a copy on the internet. In the manual you will find instructions for how to adjust the thread tension – it often goes a bit wrong after a few years of use.

CHANGE THE SEWING MACHINE NEEDLE

Sometimes the needle may have become bent, which can cause it to catch on the bobbin case or on the throat plate. The needle may also have become dull if you have been sewing over dressmaking pins, for example, and it will punch a hole in the fabric instead of piercing through it.

RE-THREAD THE SEWING MACHINE

Look in the manual or find a video on the internet to find instructions for how your particular machine should be threaded. Perhaps the thread has accidentally come off an important hook? That's often the reason for the thread becoming tangled.

CLEAN UNDER THE THROAT PLATE

There are usually little notches on the throat plate where you can insert a screwdriver and lift it up, and sometimes it is screwed into place. Either way, remove it and check if dust and scraps have gathered underneath it. It's a good idea to vacuum clean the area as best you can.

CHECK THE BOBBIN CASE

Take out the bobbin case and check if fluff has gathered where it has been sitting (usually this will happen if you have been sewing for a while). Check that no thread fibres have become stuck in the bobbin case.

CHANGE BOBBIN

For modern sewing machines, the bottom thread bobbins are made from plastic, and I have noticed that they often get nicks in them after you have been using them for a few years. Change to a bobbin that is completely new and see if that solves your problem.

OIL THE SEWING MACHINE

If you don't know when your sewing machine was last oiled, it's probably time to do it. On older machines there are usually clearly marked holes where you should add a drop of oil, but for newer machines you might need to look in the manual to see where the oil should be applied. Note that there is special sewing machine oil – don't use cooking oil!

BEFORE YOU START SEWING

Some fabrics will shrink in the wash; therefore it's a good idea to wash them before you start sewing. Before you put the fabric in the washing machine, zigzag the edges of the fabric so that they don't fray in the wash. Wash at the same temperature as you will use in the future and you will avoid any unpleasant surprises.

SECURE THE THREAD

When sewing you usually secure the thread in place at the beginning and end of the seam by sewing back and forth a few stitches; 3–4 stitches is usually enough. This will prevent the seam from unravelling.

USE ALL-PURPOSE SEWING THREAD

Only use suitable sewing thread in your machine: leave the heavy-duty hand-sewing thread be. If you want to make a seam extra strong, you can sew it twice in the same place.

Sew a pillowcase

Sewing a simple pillowcase isn't particularly complicated. I like to use linen fabric that has been left over from other projects. This project is perfect when you have a piece of fabric that isn't quite big enough for a shirt.

YOU WILL NEED
- Fabric
- Sewing machine
- Sewing thread
- Scissors
- Tape measure
- Pencil or tailor's chalk to mark your hems, seams or fold lines

Get started

The pillowcase is made from one single rectangular piece of fabric that is folded in a clever way and then sewn together with two seams. The measurement of the rectangle should be twice the width of the pillow by the length of the pillow plus the seam allowances and hems. I add another 30cm (12in) to the width to make a pocket that keeps the pillow in place inside the case.

Measure the pillow

Start by measuring the length and the width of your pillow. This case is to fit a pillow that measures 50 x 60cm (19¾ x 23½in). Therefore the piece of fabric should measure:

Width: 60cm (23½in) + 60cm (23½in) + 30cm (12in) (pocket) + 6cm (2½in) (hem) = 156cm (61½in)
Length: 50cm (19¾in) + 3cm (1¼in) (seam allowance) = 53cm (21in)

Start sewing

Cut out the rectangle and zigzag along the long edges. Hem the short edges with a 1.5cm (⅝in) double-folded hem. Both hems should be folded towards the wrong side of the fabric.

Fold the fabric with the right sides together, then fold one of the short edges back so that 30cm (12in) of it sits above the other fabric layers. If you have done this correctly, the fabric will be folded in double layers with the wrong side out, and there will be a 30cm (12in) long section positioned to create a third layer at one side. Add a few dressmaking pins to keep the fabric edges in place, then sew seams with a 1.5cm (⅝in) seam allowance along the long edges of the pillowcase.

Turn the pillowcase so that the right side is facing outwards and the pocket is facing inwards. Insert the pillow, and you are done! Isn't it insane that people don't sew pillowcases all day long, seeing as it's such a quick make?

The pocket is folded over the side of the pillowcase that is open. Its function is to hold the pillow in place.

Sew a cushion cover

This cushion cover is kept neat with button fastenings at the back. If you sew it in a sturdy fabric it will make a perfect sofa cushion. The front includes a patchwork motif but if you like, you can use the 'flying geese' pattern from the project on page 49 on your cushion cover instead.

YOU WILL NEED

- Sewing machine
- Sewing thread
- Sewing needle
- Tape measure
- Dressmaking pins
- Scissors
- Drawing paper
- Buttons
- Braid or ribbon for the button fastenings
- Iron and ironing board
- Tape or paper glue
- Textile glue (optional)

Get started

For this cushion cover you will need one front and one back panel. Both should be the same size, with the addition that the front should have a 25cm (9¾in) long section that will become the section with buttons on it at the back when the cover is finished. The following calculations include 1.5cm (5/8in) seam allowances.

THE FRONT should be the cushion's length + 28cm (11in) by its width + 3cm (1¼in).

THE BACK should be the cushion's length + 3cm (1¼in) by its width + 3cm (1¼in).

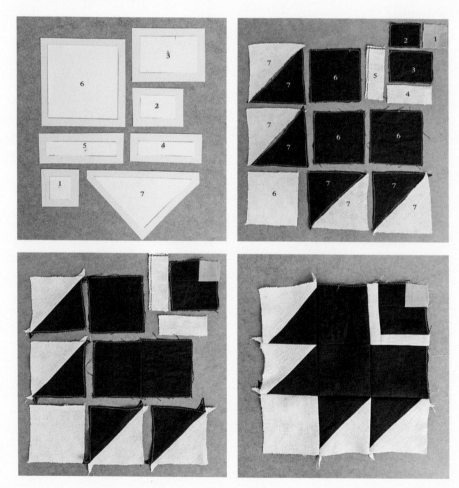

Sew the front

The blackbird motif for this cushion is sewn together from straight pieces, with straight seams. If you want to crack the code, you need to figure out in which order the pieces should be sewn together. It's a bit like a jigsaw puzzle.

This bird is made from 9 squares that are all 10 x 10cm (4 x 4in), and five of these are made up of smaller pieces. All the patchwork pieces are sewn together with a 1cm (⅜in) seam allowance. To make it easy for myself I like to draw the motif on paper, cut the pieces out and glue them to another piece of paper that I then trim to size so that I can get 1cm (⅜in) around the original piece. Then I don't have to calculate the seam allowance when I draw the pattern onto paper. Remember to add the seam allowances to the following pieces.

THE HEAD IS MADE UP OF:

1 yellow 3 x 3cm (1¼ x 1¼) square (1)
1 black 5 x 3cm (2 x 1¼in) rectangle (2)
1 black 5 x 8cm (2 x 3¼in) rectangle (3)
1 white 8 x 2cm (3¼ x ¾in) rectangle (4)
1 white 10 x 2cm (4 x ¾in) rectangle (5)

THE BODY IS MADE UP OF:

3 black 10 x 10cm (4 x 4in) squares (6)
1 white 10 x 10cm (4 x 4in) square (6)
4 black and 5 white triangles: draw a 10cm (4in) square and cut it in half diagonally for your pattern (7)

Sewing patchwork

When you have sewn two patches together press the seam allowances open at the back before you sew on the next piece. It can be helpful to lay out the pieces on the table arranged in the motif, instead of just placing them in piles that are colour co-ordinated or arranged according to another system. When the pieces are laid out in the shape they will ultimately be sewn into, it's easier to see which pieces it makes sense to sew together next.

Sew the blackbird together

Draw out all the patches on the fabric using the paper templates and tailor's chalk. Cut them out and zigzag the raw edges of the pieces.

Sew the yellow patch together with black rectangle no. 2.

Then sew on black patch no. 3, so that the yellow beak is joined to black pieces on two sides. Remember to use whatever seam allowance you added to your pattern pieces – mine is cm (⅜in).

Take the shorter of the two narrow white strips, no. 4, and sew it to the bottom along black patch no. 3. The other white strip, no. 5, is sewn to the edge that is made up of patches 2, 3, 4. Now the patch for the head is finished.

Take all the triangular pieces (7) and sew them together in pairs with one black and one white piece facing each other. Next, sew two of the large black squares (6) together.

Sew the remaining no. 6 black square to the head section along the white no. 5 piece, then sew the part that is made up of two black no. 6 patches to the head section and the black no. 6 patch that you just sewed on.

Now you will have four black and white patches, one white patch and a bird body with a head in front of you.

Sew two black and white patches together, then sew them into place to the left-hand side of the body of the bird. Sew the remaining two black and white patches to the remaining white square, then sew to the bottom edge of the bird, referring to the photographs on page 24 for positioning. The bird is finished!

The patchwork blackbird is 30cm (12in) square plus seam allowances all round. Since this is smaller than my cushion, I added a border of fabric all round. Refer back to the sizing on page 24 to calculate how large your borders should be.

Sew the cushion cover together

Zigzag the edges of the front and back pieces and hem both along the edge where you want the opening to be (the hem is folded against the wrong side of the fabric). Place the pieces with right sides together, and fold the remaining length from the longer piece so that it is sandwiched in between the front and the back pieces. (The other way around to how you sew the pillowcase project on page 19, where the pocket is placed on top.) Sew the pieces together with a 1.5cm (⅝in) seam allowance around all three sides, and leave the side where the fabric is folded over.

Sew the corners

When you sew 90-degree angles (which you usually want to do at the corners), then turn them out, it's easy to end up with cone-shaped corners and not ones as sharp as you had in mind. This is due to the seam allowances getting pushed together in the narrow corner, which bulks it out when you turn out the cushion cover.

To get nice square corners when you sew thick fabrics, you can sew a small diagonal over the corner, then cut off around half of the seam allowance. Of course, it's not risk-free to cut off the seam allowance, as the remaining fabric can start fraying. Therefore, sew the part of the seam that goes over the corner again so you have a double seam. This time you can use shorter stitches (1mm), which will usually be okay.

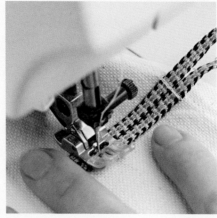

1   2

Add the case closure

I chose to make a closure with loops of braids and buttons for this case, but you can add a zip or ribbon ties if you'd prefer.

A ground rule is that a buttonhole should be the same length as the width + height of the button, so that was the measurement I used as a base when measuring my loops. I also added 8cm (3⅛in) to get a longer section above the loop. This meant my braid lengths measured twice the button width, plus twice the height of the button + 8cm (3⅛in).

I wanted three loops on my cushion, so I cut three lengths of braid and marked with a pencil where they should be positioned. To hold the braids in place while sewing it, I secured each length in place over the pencil marks with a small amount of textile glue. [1]

I fixed the loops in place by sewing back and forth four times over them with straight stitch at two points. [2]

Sew on the buttons

When the loops are in place, you can mark where you want the buttons and sew them in place, making sure each one has a shank – remember that the braid loop needs to fit underneath the button.

Start by threading a needle and tying a knot at one end of the thread. Bring up the needle from the wrong side of the fabric by the marking where

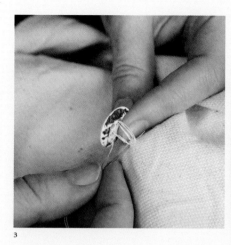

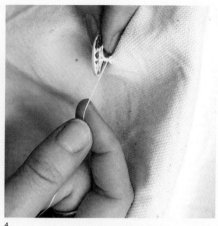

3

4

the button should sit, and pull the thread through until the knot stops it at the back of the fabric. Insert the needle through one of the holes in the button, back through another and then down through the fabric again – but place a finger between the button and the fabric so that you get a space. I like to use double sewing thread and sew the button in place with around eight stitches, at the same time as I hold the button away from the fabric with my left index finger and thumb. (3) Then I wrap the thread around six times around the stitches to hold them together. This is called the button's shank. (3, 4) Secure the thread by sewing a few stitches straight through the shank back and forth, then you can cut the thread. The cushion cover is finished!

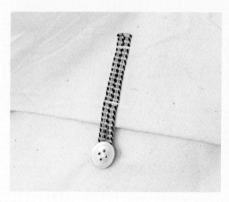

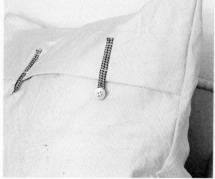

Sew a cushion cover

Sew a tote bag

As a creative person, I always carry a lot of things around, and it didn't feel all that dignified with the broken-handled blue plastic carrier bag that was my companion for many years. Eventually I got fed up and sewed myself this bag instead. It is made up of only two fabric pieces and gets its volume from its boxed corners.

YOU WILL NEED

- Sewing machine
- Sewing thread
- Fabric: heavy canvas works best
- Dressmaking pins
- Webbing or braid for handles (optional)
- Tailor's chalk or pencil
- Pattern paper
- Scissors
- Iron and ironing board

The easiest way to get a straight hem on a heavy fabric is to iron it first.

Sew a tote bag

Start by drawing out the pattern for the bag onto paper. You can draw directly onto the fabric if you want, but it's usually a good idea to start with paper to know exactly what you're doing when it's time to start cutting. Draw a square the size you want the bag to be, then add measurements for the sides and the base – which for this design have the same width. I wanted a bag with 14cm (5½in) wide sides and base, so I added 7cm (2¾in) the bottom edge and each side of the pattern. I also added a 1.5cm (⅝in) seam allowance to the sides that will be sewn together and 3cm (1¼in) at the top where the bag will be open. For example, if you want your bag to be 70 x 70cm (27½ x 27½in) and 14cm (5½in) deep, you would cut out two pieces that each measure:

WIDTH: 70cm (27½in) + 14cm (5½in) (sides) + 3cm (1¼in) for seam allowances = 87cm (34¼in)

LENGTH: 70cm (27½in) + 7cm (2¾in) (base) + 5.5cm (2⅛in) (seam allowance and hem) = 82.5cm (32⅜in)

The pattern pieces for the bag will look bigger than the dimensions of the bag when finished, but that's nothing to worry about since a part of the fabric will become the sides and base. And honestly – can a bag like this ever be too big?

Cut out the paper pattern and place it on top of the fabric, aligning the edges with the fabric grain. Mark with chalk around the paper's edges and cut out the pieces following the chalk marking.

Cut out and hem the bag pieces

Once you have cut out the bag's front and back pieces, zigzag the edges. Then make a hem on the edges that will become the top of the bag.

The easiest way to get a straight hem on a heavy fabric is to iron it first. I fold the fabric 1.5cm (⅝in) from the edge and iron until the whole edge is ironed flat against the wrong side of the fabric. Then I repeat this, folding down the edge twice, so that the first fold tucks underneath the second. When I've finished I have a razor-sharp hem that won't cause any issues. When I have ironed a hem like this, I don't use any dressmaking pins to keep it in place; I don't think it's necessary.

Sew the hem with two straight lines of stitching. I placed one line 1.3cm (½in) from the edge and the second one around 3mm (⅛in) from the edge.

Make the handles

Now it's time to add the handles. I like them long and sewn over the full length of the bag. If you don't have webbing or braid to use for handles you can make your own like this:

Cut a 9cm (3½in) wide fabric strip that is as long as you want your handle to be, plus a few centimetres for contingency. Fold the strip in half, wrong sides together, so that the long edges meet each other and iron flat. You will get a fold that runs down the middle of the whole strip; this will be your marker for this next step. Unfold the strip, fold the long edges in to meet the centre fold line and press flat with the iron. [1]

Then you can fold the strip along the middle again and iron. [2]

Now both raw edges are tucked inside the handle, which is made up of four layers of fabric. Sew the handle together by topstitching along the open edge.

1   2

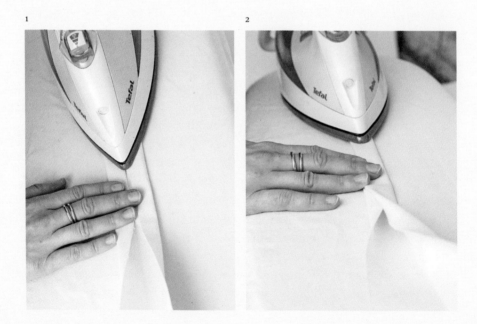

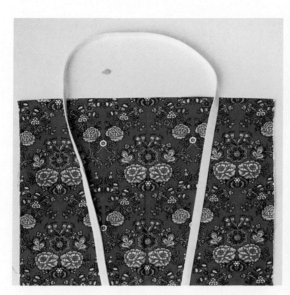

Position the handles and sew them in place

To gauge where to sew on the handles, I draw a chalk line on the fabric to mark where their edges should be positioned. I sew them on straight, placing each one so that it just covers the line. I use a small amount of textile glue to keep the handle in place instead of pins, as it's tricky to get the pin through thick layers.

Sew each handle in place 2–3mm (⅛in) from each long edge. Start at the base of the bag and sew up to the edge that will become the bag's opening. There you can reinforce the seam by sewing back and forth across the handle a few times before you continue towards the base of the bag along the second edge of the handle.

Sew the bag pieces together

When the handles are in place you can position the two bag pieces right sides facing, then sew them together using a straight seam along the three sides that aren't already hemmed. Sew with a 1.5cm (⅝in) seam allowance. When you come to the corners, you don't need to do anything in particular: just follow the edge of the fabric and continue sewing. Then you can use your iron to press the seam allowances open.

Sew a tote bag

1

2

Box the corners

Fold the corners of the bag so that the side and base seams meet, and iron flat. I decided to make the base 14cm (5½in) wide, so I needed to sew a 14cm (5½in) wide seam over the edge. Hold the tape measure by the edge and place it over the bag's side seam. Move the tape measure up and down along the folded edge until the 7cm (2¾in) mark sits over the seam when the edge of the tape measure sits over the folded edge. Draw a line across the whole corner, then sew along it with a straight seam. [3, 4]

The triangular section that you separated from the rest of the bag with a seam should now be folded in towards the base of the bag and sewn in place with a straight seam that runs along its edges. [5]

Neaten up the inside of the bag

Now we have a functional bag! To neaten it inside we will now cover the seam allowances with a strip of fabric; this will also make the bag sturdier.

Cut a 6cm (2⅜in) wide fabric strip long enough to cover both side seams and the base seam + 5cm (2in) seam allowance. Iron the edges 1cm (⅜in) along the long sides of the strip. Turn the bag inside out and place the strip over the pressed-open seam allowances. I fixed the strip in place using a small amount of textile glue, and when I came to the top edge of the bag, I folded in the short edge of the strip to prevent it from sticking out over the edge. [6] Then I sewed the strip in place by topstitching along its edges. [7]

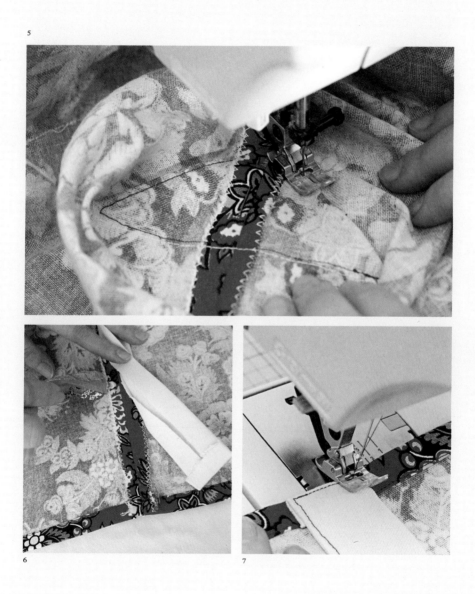

Sew a cap

This cap has a soft brim, which means you can fold it and put it in your pocket when you're not wearing it, and it can be machine washed if needed. The brim is fairly short, which is necessary when it's not supported by a plastic or card frame. I think it gives it a look somewhere between sassy and silly! In other words, perfect. I like to fold the brim so that it points slightly upwards, but for maximum sun protection you should of course have it folded down over your eyes.

YOU WILL NEED
- Sewing machine
- Sewing thread
- Scissors
- Dressmaking pins
- Pen
- Tailor's chalk
- Fabric (30 x 150cm (12 x 59in) is plenty)
- Iron and ironing board

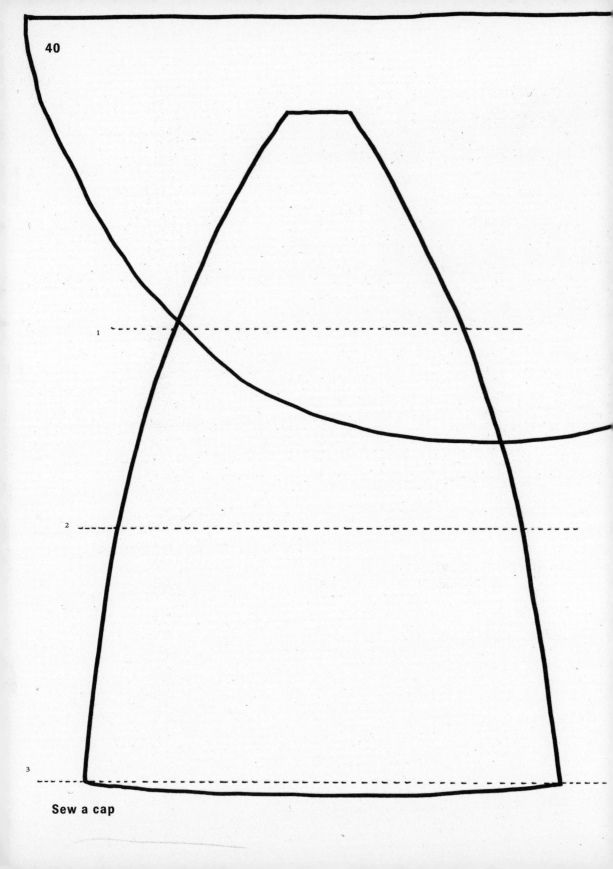

1

2

3

Sew a cap

Choose the fabric

I used a fairly sturdy fabric for my cap; I think it was meant for upholstery. Avoid using thin fabrics – old shirts or sheets, for example – as they will be too flimsy for this project. However, you could iron on fusible interlining to the back to make the material firmer.

Get started

Trace or copy the pattern pieces for the cap and draw six wedges and two brim pieces on the wrong side of the fabric using tailor's chalk. You don't need to add on a seam allowance to this pattern, as 1cm (⅜in) is already included. Also cut out a strip of fabric measuring 4 x 70cm (1½ x 27½in).

Adjust the pattern

The pattern is made to fit a head circumference of 56cm (22in). If you have a larger or smaller head, you can adjust the pattern by making the wedges wider or narrower. If there is only a minor difference, it's not worth making changes to the pattern; instead, sew 1mm inside or outside the chalked line to make the cap smaller or larger.

If the difference is 2.5cm (1in) or more, you can adjust the pattern as follows. Divide the difference between your head circumference and 56 by 12. If the difference is 2.5cm (1in), add approximately 2mm to the sides of the wedge-shaped pieces. Trace the wedge onto paper, then draw a dot on line 1. (See the illustrations overleaf.) The dot should be placed 2mm outside the wedge's line. Do the same on line 2. Also draw a dot where line 3 cuts the line of the wedge.

Now join together your three dots with a line; this line marks the new edge of the wedge. Repeat for the other side. Now the wedge is a little larger. You can make it smaller by removing instead of adding material.

Sew a cap

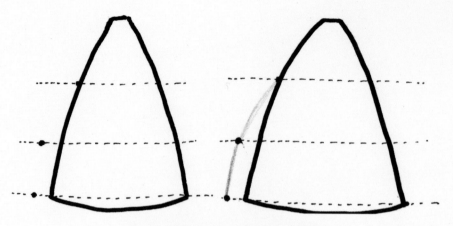

Sew the crown together

Cut out all the pieces and zigzag the wedges. (1) Take two wedges, place them with right sides together, and pin. (2) Then sew them together along one of the long edges. Fold out the two pieces and press the seam allowance open. Then finger-press both seam allowances to the left. Pin in place so that they can't unfold. Using the sewing machine stitch just to the left of the seam that holds the two pieces together. (3) This way you will secure the seam allowances on the back in place.

Sewing down the seam allowances helps to strengthen the seam and define the round shape of the cap. This type of stitching is called topstitching. It has mainly a decorative purpose that will give the cap a nicer finish.

Sew on another wedge in the same way. Then take the remaining three pieces and sew them together so that you end up with two large pieces made out of three wedges each. Place these pieces with right sides together and sew them together the same way as before, finishing off with topstitching. The result will be a round bowl of fabric that hopefully fits your head; this is the crown of the cap.

Sew the brim

Take out the pieces for the brim and their pattern. You will need three extra brim pieces that will sit inside the brim to reinforce it. Since they won't be visible, they can be cut from another fabric; I cut out pieces from

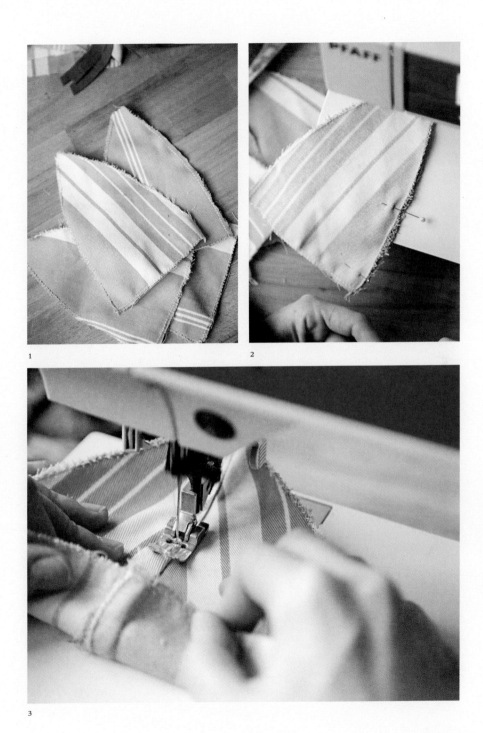

1

2

3

Sew a cap

Sew the three smaller pieces to one of the brim piece's wrong sides.

Cut down the brim's seam allowance when you have sewn together its front and back sides.

Sew a cap

a pair of worn-out dungarees. Draw out three brim pieces and cut them out, but cut off 1cm (⅜in) all round each one, because here we don't want any seam allowances.

Place the three pieces on top of each other and then centre them on top of the wrong side of one of the brim pieces. Secure properly in place with dressmaking pins through all layers of fabric, and sew them together by topstitching close to the edge of the reinforcing fabric pieces (see the photo opposite).

Finish the brim

Take both brim pieces, pin with right sides together, and sew together along the brim's curved outer edge. Then cut off around half of the seam allowance along the outer edge to ensure you get a nicer edge when you turn the brim out. (5)

Strengthen the brim with topstitches

Now sew seams through all layers of the brim to make it sturdier. Turn the brim out so that the right sides are facing out and iron it flat. Place a few pins through all layers and topstitch along the outside edge 2–3mm from the edge. Continue to cover the surface of the brim with rows of topstitching fairly close together. They can have any shape, but I chose to follow the round shape of the brim and sewed curved seams placed about half a presser foot apart. (See picture 4 overleaf.) You can of course draw them out with tailor's chalk before you sew if you want; I just improvised a little.

Sew the brim to the crown

Sew the brim to the crown with right sides together. Next, take out that long fabric strip that you cut out at the beginning. Place it wrong side up on an ironing board and fold one of the long edges, approximately 1cm (⅜in) to the wrong side, and press down. Now, pin the unfolded long edge of the strip to the edge of the crown, right sides together, with the brim in between the strip and the crown. I let the start and the end of the strip meet at the centre back of the cap. (It's good to have a 2cm (¾in) of the strip spare at both ends, so you can fold them over each other later.) Sew the strip on (and the brim that sits in place underneath it) with a 1cm (⅜in) seam allowance. (5) Where the strip ends and starts, I sew as close to the ends as possible, without the seams overlapping.

Fold the strip towards the inside of the cap

Finally, fold the strip towards the crown of the cap and pin it in place. Can you see that the edge that you pressed down on the strip before is now neatly positioned inwards? Pin it in place. At the middle of the back, fold one part of the strip over the other, so that no raw edges are visible. (6)

Sew the strip in place

Now you need to sew the strip in place. This is done by topstitching from the right side of the cap. It can feel strange to sew something in place that you can't see, but it will be fine! Place the first line of topstitching just inside the edge of the crown, then place one more around 1.5cm (⅝in) up from the edge. (7) Since the strip on the back is 2cm (¾in) wide, these topstitches will hold it in place and give additional strength to the edge.

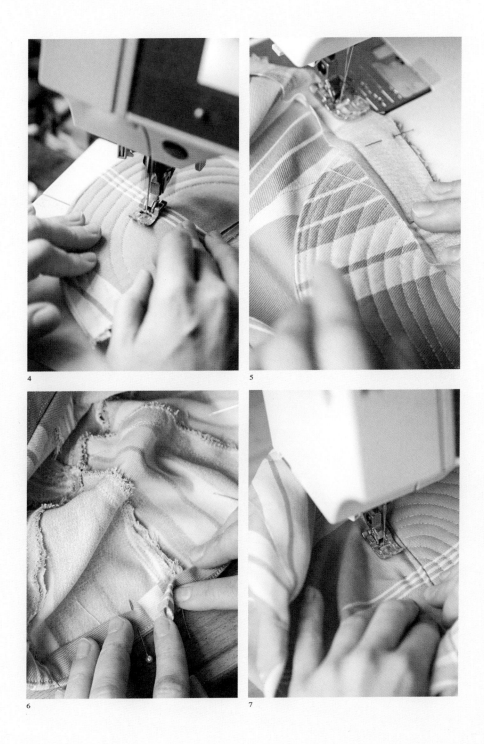

4

5

6

7

Sew a cap

Sew a patchwork quilt

Sewing a patchwork quilt can be time-consuming and complicated, but it can also be simple. This version takes only a few evenings to make. I chose not to be too meticulous with the measurements, so the pattern became a bit wonky. It gives the piece a lively feel, I think! This is my version of a classic quilting pattern called 'flying geese', which got its name from the triangles that resemble birds in flight.

YOU WILL NEED

- Fabric for the quilt's front and back
- Wadding
- Card and pen
- Tailor's chalk
- Sewing machine and sewing thread
- Dressmaking pins
- Sewing needle + thread for quilting
- Scissors
- Iron and ironing board

Get started

Start by sourcing fabric for your patchwork quilt. If you don't have a stash of fabrics to hand, you can visit a flea market and buy some old linen or something similar. The indigo blue cotton and madder red silk fabric that I used were scrap pieces left over from other projects. For patchwork quilts I only use woven fabrics with no stretch.

Draw templates

The first thing I do when making a patchwork quilt is to draw out the pattern pieces on sturdy card. In this case, only two pieces are needed: one large isosceles triangle (13cm (5in) wide and 8cm (3⅛in) high) and one smaller triangle made by drawing a triangle the same size as the larger one and then cutting it in half vertically. The smaller pieces will be placed at the edges to make these straight. Make sure to add a seam allowance to your templates – I added 1cm (⅜in) all round.

Cut out the triangles

Draw out the pattern pieces on the fabric and cut them out. It's handy if all the pieces have the grain going the same way. I prefer the grain line to run along the base of the triangle.

You can calculate how many pieces you will need by comparing the size of the patchwork quilt you want to make with the size of the pieces. I used 90 large triangles and 20 small ones, and my patchwork quilt ended up 66 x 82cm (26 x 32¼in). This was a suitable size to make a present for a small child or perhaps to use as a wall hanging.

Sew the patches together to form horizontal strips

When the pieces have been cut out it's time to start sewing. First I laid out all the pieces on the floor to see where I wanted to place the red triangles. Now is the time to find out if you have cut out enough pieces or if you want to cut out some more in a specific colour.

When you are happy with your composition, gather the pieces into small piles made up of all the pieces that will form one horizontal strip in the patchwork quilt. My rows were made up of nine large pieces and two small ones.

Now sew the pieces together to form long horizontal strips. Each strip starts and finishes with one small triangle, and it's important to keep the top and bottom edges of the strips as even as possible. They can differ by a few millimetres, but preferably no more than 5mm (¼in) if you, like me, are working with a 1cm (⅜in) seam allowance. If the fabric has a right side and a wrong side, place the right sides together. In the beginning it can be tricky to work out how to place the triangles over each other to make sure they are positioned correctly, but keep in mind that the pieces should be placed so that the seam, which runs 1cm (⅜in) from the edge, starts and finishes where the two fabric pieces meet. This means they should be placed edge to edge, but slightly shifted in relation to each other where you sew them together. Look carefully at illustration 2 and you'll see what I mean.

You don't need to zigzag

When sewing clothes, you would usually zigzag the edges of the pieces to prevent them from fraying, but I don't usually do this when sewing patchwork quilts. All fabric edges will end up inside the quilt anyway, and there they won't be subject to much wear and tear.

Sew the pieces together to form horizontal strips

Sew a patchwork quilt

Sew the pieces together to form horizontal strips

When you have sewn all the pieces together, press the seams open as best you can. Some seam allowances will be sewn down at the back, so you won't be able to press them open, but that's okay. Iron them as flat as possible. Keep in mind that if you have used any synthetic fabric (polyester, acrylic, etc) you need to be careful with the heat on the iron so the fabric doesn't melt.

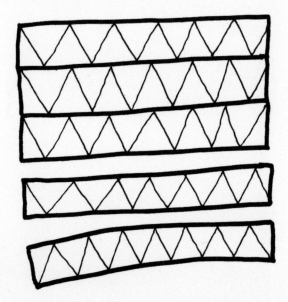

Sew the strips together to form one piece

Now you can sew all the horizontal strips together to make one large piece. I sew on one strip at a time instead of pinning together all of the strips in one go; it's easier that way. When all the strips are sewn together with horizontal seams, the front is finished. You can press the seam allowances open and start working on the back.

The back

My back piece consists of a linen napkin woven by a dear friend, my grandma's old monogrammed tea towel and a few pieces of indigo-dyed fabric.

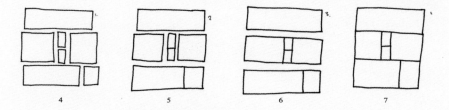

They are all sewn together with straight seams and the seam allowances have been ironed open at the back. I always make the back piece slightly larger than the front piece, as it will be easier to line the pieces up that way. You can of course use a whole piece of fabric if you prefer.

Quilt the layers

Lay out your back piece, face down, place the wadding on top and then pin the patchwork, face up, on top. Now it's time to secure all the pieces together. This is what's called quilting. I sew straight rows of seams by hand along the whole patchwork quilt – you can use a sewing machine, but I think that's tricky, so prefer sewing by hand. I draw out the lines with tailor's chalk before I start sewing. My favourite thread to use is 35/2 linen thread that I wax by running the thread over a piece of beeswax a few times.

I work tiny backstitches that are widely spaced, as shown in the photograph on page 56. The stitches should go through all the layers of fabric and will keep the wadding in place. I sewed lines along the pattern on the front, but you can sew any pattern you want as long as there is no more than 12cm (4¾in) in between the rows of stitches. When you have finished, you can trim the edges of the patchwork quilt around the front fabric so that all three layers are the same size and no layer protrudes more than the others.

Bind the edges

The last thing to do is to sew on a binding. I think it looks nice if the binding is under 2cm (¾in) wide, but that is a matter of taste. Cut out a strip that is twice as wide as you want the binding to be plus the seam allowance

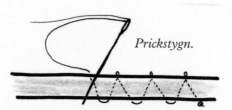

Prickstygn.

x 2, and long enough to go around the whole patchwork quilt with a little bit of safety margin. I sew the binding on using the sewing machine, right sides facing the right side of the patchwork quilt and 1.5cm (⅝in) in from the edge. Start by sewing the binding in the middle of one of the long sides and pin in place until the first corner. When you come to

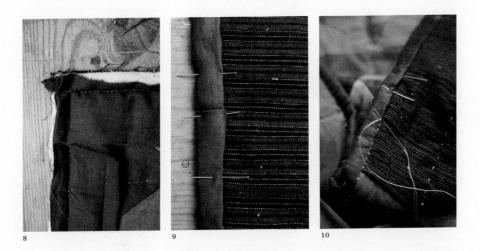

8   9   10

the corner you can secure the thread 1.5cm (⅝in) from the edge and fold the binding. Then you sew along the next side, starting at the quilt edge, which will secure the fold in place. This way you will get a neat corner. (8)

Sew the binding in place at the back

When you come to the end of the binding, let it overlap with the start of it and fold the end in so that the raw edge isn't visible. The last step is to sew the binding down at the back. I do this by hand using small stitches that catch the fabric on the back but that don't go through to the fabric on the front. I pin the binding tightly around the edge and fold it as I go along while I sew it in place so that it just covers the seam it's sewn on with. (9) This way the edge will become slightly rounded, which will give the impression of a well-padded quilt. (10)

When the patchwork quilt is finished it's good to wash it once to get rid of any chalk residue and to make the different fabrics come together nicely. I always wash my patchwork quilts using the wool programme on the washing machine, as I worry that the wadding will shrink if I use anything more vigorous. Let the quilt dry as flat as possible.

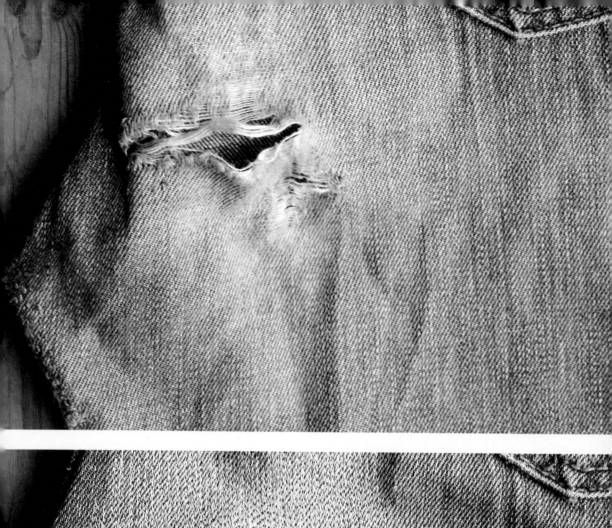

Mend jeans on a sewing machine

Visible mending is fantastic, but it has its time and place. Jeans often wear out in the crotch, and that might not be the place where you want a funny character or some graphic embroidery. With discreet mending it's quite quick to restore a pair of jeans to make them wearable again. You can of course mend by hand; if you want to do this, try using a soft cotton yarn rather than sewing thread. I prefer to use 8/2 cotton weaving yarn but you could also buy embroidery thread in your local yarn shop, and it will work just as well.

YOU WILL NEED
- Sewing machine
- Sewing thread
- Mending patch
- Scissors
- Textile glue
- Iron and ironing board

Choose a mending fabric

Mending jeans with denim fabric might seem logical, but in reality it doesn't work very well. The mend will be twice as thick as the fabric around the patch, which can make the garment uncomfortable. I only mend with denim fabric if a large part of the fabric of the jeans has worn away and a gaping hole needs to be completely replaced. However, usually the garment is only worn thin with a rip in the most fragile place, so a patch made from cotton fabric – from a discarded shirt, for example – will work best.

Choose a sewing thread

I usually use Gütermann's sewing thread in colour 68 when I mend jeans. It's a very neutral colour that goes towards grey. It doesn't stand out colour-wise, but blends nicely into the surrounding colours. It's only if the jeans are very light or very dark that I change colour. In general, it's good to choose a less intense colour for the mending thread than the garment's original colour if you want to make an invisible mend.

How large is the hole?

First inspect the damage on the garment. It often looks worse than it actually is. A good trick is to hold the fabric up against the light; then you will see which parts have worn out and become fragile.

Secure the mending patch

When I mend jeans, I place the worn-out part on an ironing board and flatten out the fabric around the hole. The aim is to position the fabric with the grain despite it being ripped. If you want, you can iron to smooth out the fabric. If the hole is large, it can be good to pin the fabric to the ironing board so that it is completely still. Now you can see the shape of the hole, you can work out how large the mending patch needs to be.

I make my patch around 1cm (⅜in) larger than the area to be mended (the hole + the damaged area around it) and secure it in place with small

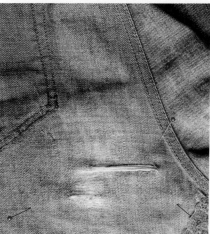

dollops of textile glue. You can use pins or basting thread if you prefer, but I think textile glue works best.

The glue is not a part of the mending; it's just to secure the patch in place before you sew it on. Too much glue will turn the mend to a hard disc. In the worst-case scenario, the glue will leak through the fabric and leave ugly stains on the front of the garment, so be careful with this step. When the patch is glued into position on the inside of the garment and the glue has dried you can remove the garment from the ironing board and turn it out so that you see the right side.

If there are a lot of loose threads hanging around the hole you can cut them off, although I think the mending is better if you save as much original material as possible. I usually take a small amount of glue on my fingers, run it behind the loose edges, then press them against the mending patch.

Before you start sewing

Thread the sewing machine with the same colour for the top and bottom thread. Place the work with the right side up so that the left edge of the hole is positioned by the needle and lower the presser foot. The key to making a mend that looks invisible is to sew dense rows of stitches by first sewing forwards and then reversing back over the hole. The stitches should cover the whole surface where the mending patch is positioned at the back of the garment.

I usually place my stitches in line with the fabric's blue threads, but you can also place the rows of stitches in line with the fabric's twill line – the diagonal lines that are a typical feature of jeans. I don't tend to sew across the blue threads in the denim fabric since the sewing thread will then sit over them instead of in between them, which makes the mending much more visible.

Sewing the mend

Cover the whole area with stitches from left to right by sewing forwards and then reversing with the sewing machine. You can secure the thread at the beginning and the end by reversing a little and then going forward, but you should secure it ahead of starting a new row: just pull the fabric a millimetre to the left and then start reversing. The rows of stitches don't have to cross over each other, and you can simply use straight stitch. Try to resist the temptation of using zigzag! Straight stitch is perfectly adequate and will blend into the fabric's structure much better. When the whole surface is covered in stitches you can go back and sew an extra layer on top of the area that was most worn out if you want. Then you're finished!

Sew straight rows of stitches that cover the whole area that you want to mend. Alternate between sewing forwards and reversing.

The damaged area is fully covered in stitches.

Mend jeans on a sewing machine

Dye wool yarn with birch leaves

Most plants can be used for dyeing, but not all colours will stand up to sunlight or washing. Birch leaves are a classic for this context since they are easy to obtain and produce a bright yellow colour that is fairly durable. Dyeing with plants isn't actually that difficult. You place the plants in hot water and leave them to release the dye; then you add fabric or yarn to soak up the dye.

YOU WILL NEED
- Large stainless-steel pot (not one you use for food)
- Alum (15g per 100g yarn, or ½oz per 3½oz)
- Birch leaves
- Wool yarn
- Yarn in contrasting colour for tying
- Thermometer (optional)

Prepare the yarn

If you add a ball of yarn to the pot, only the outer layer will pick up the dye, since the dye bath will struggle to soak all the way into the centre of the ball. Therefore, the yarn needs to be wound into a hank so that the dye can reach every part of the yarn. If you don't have a so-called 'niddy noddy', you can wind the yarn around the back of a chair.

Tie the ends of the yarn together and also tie a few lengths of yarn in a strongly contrasting colour loosely around the hank. The ties will prevent the hank from getting tangled, which otherwise happens very easily when it is placed into the dye bath. Four ties are usually enough, but you can make more. If you tie tightly with the contrasting yarn, you will get lighter patches in that spot, since the dye won't be able to soak through there. If you want an even colour you can tie with loose loops so the yarn can move around a little.

It can be a good idea to wash the yarn before you dye it. Use specific wool detergent and lukewarm water.

Dye wool yarn with birch leaves

A hank of yarn.

Good to know

When dyeing wool yarn it is important not to shock it with the temperature of the water, since that can cause the yarn to felt. If I need to place yarn in a pot with hot water I do it in stages: first I soak the yarn in lukewarm water in a separate pot, then change to slightly warmer water, and then a little warmer again before using proper hot water. Now the yarn will have about the same temperature as the dye bath and you can add it in. After the dyeing it's good to leave the yarn to cool in the pot with the dye bath overnight.

The yarn must be able to move freely in the pot: if it's tightly packed, the dye will bond unevenly and the yarn will come out blotchy. Stir the pot multiple times during the dyeing process so that the dye penetrates everywhere. Stirring too vigorously can cause the yarn to felt, however, so take it easy.

Treat the yarn with a mordant

Most plant dyes will become stronger and more defined if you pre-treat the yarn with a mordant, a method that makes the yarn more receptive to dye pigments. The naturally occurring mineral salt alum is one of the most common mordants used when dyeing protein fibres such as wool and silk.

Place the yarn in a pot filled with lukewarm water. Heat up the yarn until it's simmering but not boiling. In a cup, weigh out 15g (½oz) of alum per 100g (3½oz) of yarn to be dyed. Add a little warm water to the cup to dissolve the alum, then pour the solution into the pot with the yarn. Now keep it at simmering point around 90° C (194° F) for 1 hour. After this the yarn can be rinsed and dried or dyed straight away.

Dye wool yarn with birch leaves

Dyeing

Bring birch leaves to the boil in enough water to cover them. A good rule of thumb is 1kg (2.2lb) of fresh leaves per 1kg (2.2lb) when it comes to amounts, although I usually go for 'the more the better' since I like strong colours. Leave the leaves to boil for at least 1 hour, preferably 3, before you strain them out of the dye bath and lower in the yarn that you can then leave to simmer for at least 1 hour. Avoid boiling the yarn, as that will increase the chance of it felting.

When the yarn is taken out of the pot it will need a thorough rinse. Fill a bucket with water the same temperature as the dye bath (that is, hot, if you take it out of a simmering pot). Leave the yarn for a few minutes, stir carefully, and then change the water. Repeat until the water no longer runs yellow. A dash of vinegar in one of the rinse baths is good, as it will make the yarn a bit shinier and will help fix the dye.

PS: Ask the landowner for permission before picking fresh birch leaves.

Dye wool yarn with birch leaves

Darn a sock

Few things make me feel as wholesome as darning woolly socks. I don't usually bother with standard cotton socks, but you could certainly mend them too. The expression 'to darn' is used when you cover a hole in a garment with a series of stitches that are placed so that you build up a new 'fabric'.

YOU WILL NEED
- Darning needle
- Darning mushroom or similar
- Yarn for mending
- Scissors

Darn a sock

Stretch the work

When darning by hand, it's easy to pull the yarn too tightly; therefore, you usually stretch the garments over something when darning them. There are specific tools for this that are called darning mushrooms; they look a bit like a mushroom made from wood. If you don't have one of those you can use a tennis ball or a similar bulbous object. The main consideration is that you can stretch the part that you are mending onto something. I used the lid from a thermos flask that I put inside of the sock, then tied a band around it to keep the lid in place.

Choose a yarn

I prefer to mend wool garments with wool yarn and cotton garments with cotton yarn, but there are a few exceptions. Many modern wool garments are given a superwash treatment that makes them machine-washable. Then it's best to mend them with a wool yarn that is superwash-treated, otherwise the mending will shrink when you wash the garment. You can also use cotton yarn for superwash-treated garments, since it doesn't tend to shrink in the wash.

How much should be mended?

When mending clothes, it's good to check if the area around the hole is worn or not. If it's a heel or a toe on a sock, for example, the area around the hole is usually worn out as well, so you might as well mend everything that is about to tear at the same time. I usually make the mending larger than the actual hole, since I don't want a hole to appear right next to the mending immediately after I have mended a pair of socks.

Thread the needle

It can be difficult to get the end of a fluffy wool yarn through the eye of a needle, so try the following. Fold the yarn around the eye of the needle and press down with your fingers to make it taut. [1] Pull out the needle and push the little folded loop you're pressing together through the eye of the needle. [2]

1   2

Secure the yarn

Secure the yarn by sewing through a few stitches, then turn and sew back the same way through the adjacent stitches. (3, 4) This way you will avoid bulky knots that will be uncomfortable to walk on.

Mark the area to be mended

Sew a ring with standard up-and-down stitches (running stitch) around the hole. (5) This ring will serve as extra reinforcement at the edge of the mending and will prevent the hole from stretching and becoming larger as you mend it.

Start darning

Broadly speaking, the actual darning is done by sewing in threads over the hole so that it's covered; then you sew in more threads at a 90-degree angle to the first.

In the first step, you sew from side to side over the hole. Insert the needle just outside the ring of stitches that you sewed around the hole. Pick up a thread in the sock and come out with the needle straight away. All jumps over the hole with the yarn should be made from the outside of the sock. (6)

3

4

5

6

Darning tips

There are a few things you need to keep in mind. The yarn you're sewing with needs to sit fairly loosely over the hole; there needs to be enough of it to go over and under the yarn in the second layer later on; and if you pull it tight at this stage, the mending will pull together too much later on.

You will need to sew the stitches fairly densely – often more densely than you might think. (7)

If you want to change colour, secure the yarn in the same manner as when you started: by sewing a few stitches first in one direction and then in the other direction. Then you can secure the new colour the same way and continue mending.

Darn a sock

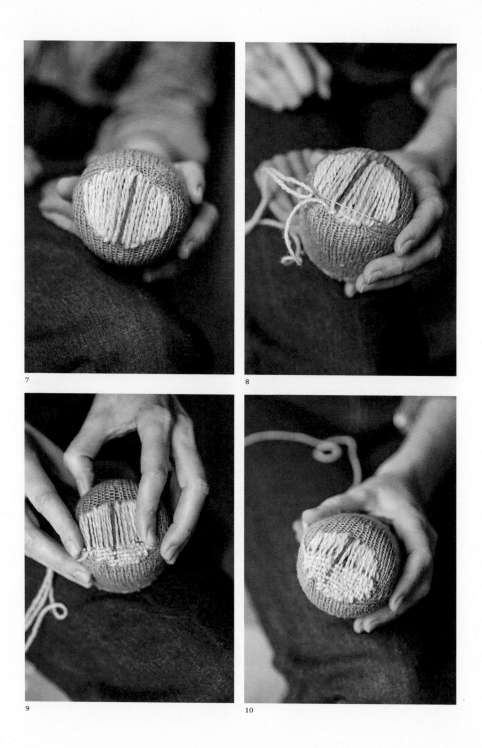

7

8

9

10

Darn a sock

I made the stitches at the sides shorter than those that run over the middle of the hole, since I wanted the finished mending to be in the shape of a circle.

Get weaving

Now we need to sew stitches in the other direction so that the threads form a weave. [8] The principle of sewing stitches from one edge to the other still applies, but now you insert the needle in between the previous threads. Run the needle under one thread and over the next until you reach the other side. Then secure the yarn around one of the sock's stitches and turn back. Now you go over the threads you just went under, and vice versa. If possible, insert the needle and pick all the threads to be picked up before you pull the needle and thread through.

Here you also need to make fairly dense stitches, so it's good to pack the yarn together by pushing the needle against the previous 'row'. [9]

It's easy to get out of step and accidentally pick up the wrong thread or pick up two threads at the same time. It usually doesn't matter too much. Just continue sewing and pretend it never happened; you probably won't be able to see it when it's finished anyway.

Finish the mending

When you decide that the mending is finished, secure the yarn as I described earlier by sewing back and forth. Take out the darning mushroom, thermos lid, or whatever you used to stretch the sock, and then you're done!

Mend knitwear with embroidery

When the elbows of my favourite cardigan started to wear thin and also had some ugly stains, I decided to kill two birds with one stone by reinforcing the elbows and at the same time covering the stain with embroidery that looks like part of the knitting.

YOU WILL NEED
- Yarn for mending, thinner than the yarn of the garment
- Large-eyed needle

Before you start

This technique involves sewing stitches that look like knitted stitches over the existing stitches on a knitted garment. It is therefore perfect to reinforce garments that are about to tear. It's a little bit like colouring in: the basic structure is already there, then you sew with new yarn over the old.

To avoid the mending becoming too thick I used a yarn that was about half the thickness of the yarn from which the garment was made. I prefer to use a 2-ply yarn, since single-stranded yarn has a tendency to break off as you work with it.

Draw out your pattern

If you don't want the mending to be very visible you can choose yarn in the same colour as the garment, but I chose to embroider a carnation pattern inspired by a Fair Isle design. I drew the pattern on squared paper so I could refer to a clear chart. One square on the paper corresponds to one stitch in the garment, but since the stitches on my garment aren't completely square, the motif ended up slightly stretched widthways.

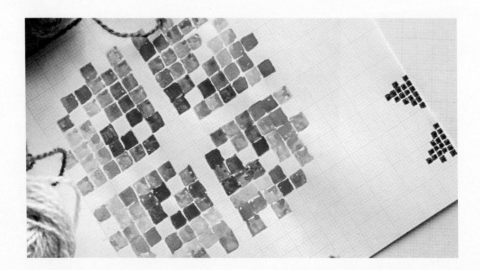

Mend knitwear with embroidery

Where to position the mending?

To check where to place the mending, I put on the cardigan and checked where it was most worn. In the middle of the worn area over the elbow I picked out one stitch that I marked by tying a length of blue yarn around it. The carnation on my chart has a middle made up of nine empty squares, and I decided that the middle square should correspond to the middle stitch on my cardigan.

Secure the yarn

I secured the yarn by sewing through a few stitches on the inside of the sleeve, then turning and sewing back the same way through the adjacent stitches. This way you can avoid lumpy knots at the back of the mending.

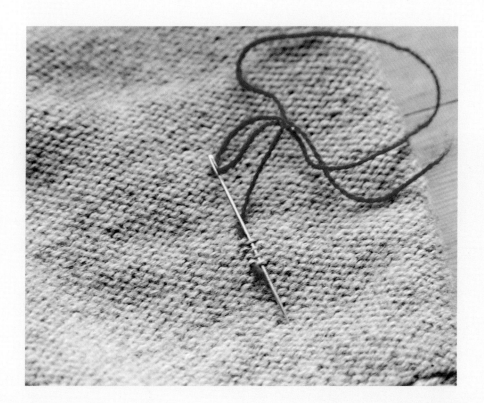

Mend knitwear with embroidery

Sew duplicate stitch

When you have secured the yarn you can bring the needle up through the first stitch you want to fill in. Follow the direction of the yarn upwards in an arch, under the stitch above and then down again so you can insert the needle in the same place where it came up. [1, 2] Pull just enough so that the embroidery yarn sits softly over the stitch of the garment; no tighter than that. It's important to be gentle when sewing duplicate stitch, otherwise the stitches won't fill out the surface they are intended to cover. I prefer to sew my stitches from right to left or downwards. If I sew from left to right or upwards, they don't look as nice.

Fill in the pattern

With the stitch marked in blue as a starting point, I began to sew my red carnation. I used a dark red yarn for the middle of the petals' inner parts and a bright red yarn for the outer parts [3]; then I filled in the background. When you've run out of thread and you need to secure it you can do it the same way as when you started sewing: by sewing a couple of stitches through the knitted stitches at the back of the garment.

Add some steam

When you have finished sewing you can iron over the new reinforcement with an iron on a low temperature and with a lot of steam. This makes the wool yarn relax a little and makes the surface more even. Avoid pressing hard with the iron; instead, hold it slightly above the surface of the garment so that the yarn has a chance to move slightly. Placing a damp cloth between the garment and the iron guarantees that you don't accidentally get any burn marks, or that the iron leaves any other ugly stains. Your decorative mend should now meld seamlessly into the knitting of your garment. [4]

1

2

3

4

Mend knitwear with embroidery

Himmeli

Several basic shapes in different sizes are put together here to make a feather-light mobile that can hang over a festive table setting, or even above your bed. In Finland and eastern Europe, this type of decoration is traditionally made from rye straw, but my version is made from last season's grass that I picked during the winter. I look for thick straws and use the sturdier parts that give the himmeli a shimmer with their subtle golden sheen.

YOU WILL NEED
- Scissors
- Darning needle / thick needle
- Sturdy hollow grass stems
- Liquid glue
- Sewing thread
- Pom poms or other decorations

To make all straws the same length I cut one measuring straw as a template.

Gather the grass straws

Start by gathering grass straws for your himmeli. Bring a pair of scissors when you go for a walk and look for long, thick straws amid last season's grass. You want the stalks that stand straight and that have little nodes, a bit like bamboo. It's only the part furthest down towards the ground that is thick enough to use for himmeli, so cut the straw as close to the ground as possible. The straw should be hollow and wide enough so that you can get a darning needle through it without a problem.

Often there will be a soft outer coating of brown-grey grass that can usually be removed after some picking; you will find the golden part inside. I prefer to cut off the parts that have been exposed to weather and wind, since they are often more matte and greyer than the surface that has been protected by a layer of grass. Cut the grass into pieces by the nodes, where the straw isn't hollow; those parts you might as well remove straight away.

Prepare the straws

Once you're back home, you can soak the grass straws in warm water for 15 minutes to make them easier to handle. Dry straws crack easily when you cut them into pieces.

For my himmeli I made one single basic bipyramidal shape, but with varying proportions. For each basic shape I used 16 longer pieces and 8 short ones. There are no specific measurements you need to stick to, but a good guideline is that the shorter pieces should be two-thirds the length of the long pieces. To get all straws the same size I cut a measuring straw that I used as a template when cutting the rest.

Put together a basic shape

Start by cutting an arm's length of thread and thread it on to the needle. I used Bockens 60/2 twine, a linen thread that is very nice to work with since it's not slippery. Standard sewing thread will also work fine.

Thread 4 long straws onto the thread and tie the thread's ends so that the 4 straws form a rhombus. [1] If the needle doesn't go through easily, you can shake the straw upside down a little, like a ketchup bottle, and it should come through eventually.

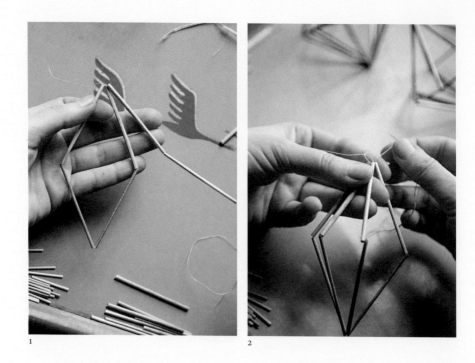

1 2

Now thread on 2 long straws and secure the thread at the bottom of the rhombus with a single knot. Continue in the same way until your basic shape has 8 'arms'. (2)

When the thread runs out

When the thread is close to running out, you can splice it as follows: Remove the thread from the needle, measure out a new length of thread and simply tie the old thread to the new one using a standard double knot. Thread the needle to the new end and continue building your himmeli. The knot on the thread will be hidden inside a straw. Cut the ends short enough that they don't protrude from the sides of the straw.

3   4

Add the shorter pieces

Now thread the needle back through one of the straws so that it comes out in the middle of an 'arm'. Thread one of the short straws onto the needle [3] and secure it to the middle of the next arm with a single knot. [4] Here you pull tightly enough so that the short straw doesn't hang loosely, but not so tight that the straw cracks. Continue until you have tied all the long arms together with short straws and finish with a double knot when you have secured the last straw. Now you have a finished basic shape.

Assemble the himmeli

My himmeli is made up of 4 basic bipyramidal shapes in different sizes that hang from each other. 8 little shapes are tied to the corners of the largest one. To join 2 shapes together you simply tie them with sewing thread and secure with a knot. I cut the ends short, just under 1cm (⅜in), then hid them by adding a small amount of glue to the darning needle and using it to push the end into a grass straw. This will leave some glue in the straw, making the end stay in place. This is easiest to do if the himmeli is hanging in the air; otherwise it's easy for your hand to slip and accidentally break something.

Finally, I decorated my himmeli with yarn pom poms by tying them on where I wanted them and hiding the ends of their threads inside the straw the same way as before.

PS: You can make your himmeli from reeds as well. Then you can make larger shapes since reed straws tend to be stronger than grass straws.

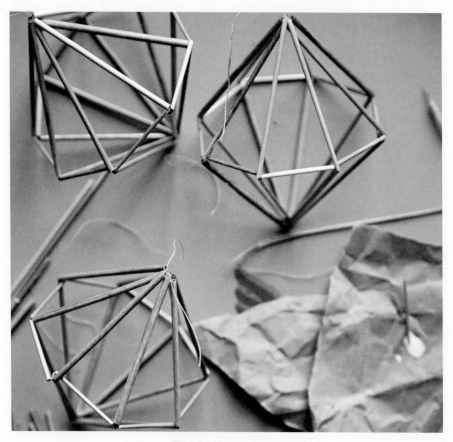

Finished basic shapes.

Embroider a fabric patch

A ripped jacket, outdated merch or a boring cap – everything is more fun with an embroidered patch! You can use patches to cover ugly stains or holes in a garment, but they can also be used to express your identity. If I owned a hot dog van, I would sell this sausage patch to my regulars!

YOU WILL NEED

- Large-eyed needle
- Standard sewing needle
- Fabric for the patch
- Yarn or thread for the embroidery
- Sewing thread for attaching the patch
- Scissors
- Pencil

Choose your fabric

I use a densely fulled wool fabric when making embroidered fabric patches as I like the way it doesn't tend to fray at the edges, but you could use a sturdy fabric made from any material. Keep in mind that if you attach the patch to something that you want to be able to wash, the material of the patch needs to be the same as the material of the garment, otherwise they might shrink at different rates. A patch made from wool fabric on a pair of exercise leggings won't look that nice after a warm wash since wool will shrink if you wash it on a normal cycle, but it goes well on a denim jacket. This is because it will only do the denim good to be washed on a wool programme!

Choose your yarn or thread

I have embroidered with 16/2 linen yarn, but you could use nearly any yarn or thread made up of two or more strands. Single-ply yarn – that is, yarn made up of only one strand – tends to break when sewing with it, so avoid this if you are a beginner. If the yarn is made from linen and fluffs a lot, as mine did, you can wax it first by running it over a piece of beeswax a couple of times.

Getting started

Start by sketching out your motif. You can draw straight onto the patch if you feel brave – a smiley isn't that complicated, after all – or make a sketch on paper first. You can use a pencil for drawing on white fabrics, as long as you only draw where you will embroider. You can buy marker pens with washable ink in craft-supply shops, if you want to be on the safe side. When I sew on black fabrics I sketch out the motif with a white eyeliner pencil from my make-up bag – it works perfectly!

I mark out the shape of the patch – a circle, in this case – but I wait until the embroidery is finished before cutting it out. If you like, you can use an embroidery hoop to stretch out the fabric. This will prevent the fabric from puckering when you embroider, but I think it's useful to learn not to pull the stitches too tightly. With a light enough touch, you won't need a hoop!

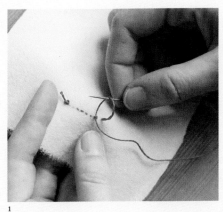
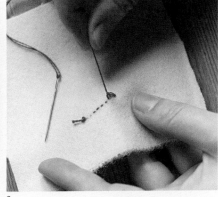

Secure the thread

My embroidered patch will be sewn onto a jacket, so there is no need to mess about with neat, invisible ways to secure the thread. When you start embroidering you can secure the thread at the back by tying a knot at one end, then thread the needle on the other end and bring the needle up from the back of the fabric. The knot will form a 'stop' that prevents the thread from coming through completely.

When you have embroidered for a while and have around 15cm (6in) left of your thread, it's time to start thinking about changing to a new length, but first you need to secure the old one. Sew a little loop around the last stitch you made at the wrong side of the work, insert the needle through the loop and pull. Often this type of knot is enough to secure the thread, but sometimes you might need to make several. [1,2]

Sew stem stitch

There are as many different embroidery stitches as there are grains of sand in the Sahara, but here I have used just one: stem stitch. As the name suggests, this is very suitable for embroidering straight lines such as flower stems; it's also useful if you want to fill large areas. When you sew stem stitches you sort of work backwards. Start by securing the thread at the wrong side of the fabric and bring the threaded needle through to the right side of the fabric. In one movement, take the needle into the fabric one stitch length ahead and bring it out halfway back along the stitch you are making. When you pull the needle through, a loop is formed that will sit on the fabric's surface as a stitch. [1] When you make the next stitch you repeat the procedure: insert the needle a few millimetres further along on your drawn line, and bring the point up right at the end of your previous stitch. [2]

The result is that every stitch tucks around the previous stitch, which makes the embroidered line look interlinked. The trick to making these stitches look neat is to always bring the needle up on the same side of the loop. Here you can see that I kept the loop to the left of the line that I was embroidering over.

I think that stem stitches look best if you make them fairly short: around 3–4mm (⅛in) is usually good depending on the thickness of the yarn.

Fill an area

When I want to cover large areas with stem stitches I sew many rows next to each other. Be extra careful when you pull the stitch so that it still sits slightly loose on top of the fabric. This is because stem stitches tend to pucker the fabric, and if you are too hard on your hands no embroidery hoop in the world will help. [3]

Attach the patch

When you have finished your embroidery you can iron the wrong side of the fabric carefully with a lot of steam if it's puckering at all, then you can cut out the patch and sew it in place where you want it. I usually use straight whipstitch here. This is a small stitch that is sewn by letting the thread run diagonally at the back of the work and straight at the front of the work. The result is small stitches that keep the patch edges in place without being very visible. [4]

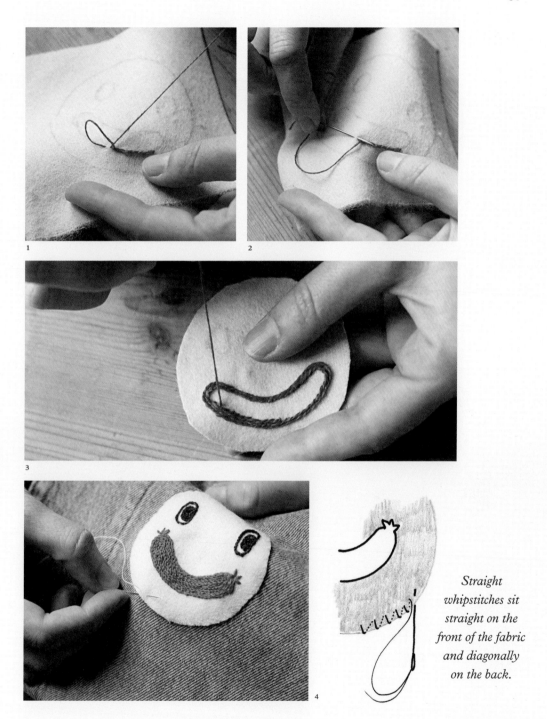

*Straight
whipstitches sit
straight on the
front of the fabric
and diagonally
on the back.*

Embroider a fabric patch

Spin yarn from wool

One of my teachers said that the simpler the tool, the more expertise you need to handle it with. This is certainly the case when spinning yarn. When you watch an experienced spinner, it looks as though the yarn simply flows out of their hands, but when you try it yourself, nothing happens. You drop the spindle, it rattles, you swear and then you have to try again. And again. But put in enough practice and you'll get the hang of it eventually.

YOU WILL NEED
- Wool
- Carders
- Spindle

Can I use any type of wool?

All wool can be spun. Some spinners even spin yarn from dog and cat hair!

I have some wool, now what?

Freshly shorn sheep's wool is often fairly dirty, so the first thing you need to do when you get a bag of raw wool is to take out the worst parts. The wool from the sheep's belly and rear is usually felted into clumps and dirty, so you don't want that. If you're able to choose, you should pick wool that has been shorn in the autumn, when the animals have been outside all summer. That's usually cleanest.

Wash the wool

You can spin the wool unwashed if you want, but I prefer to wash it first. Then you'll get rid of a lot of the dirt and the farmyard smell, and you can always save washed wool if you don't have time to spin it straight away. Storing unwashed wool in bags is not recommended; it can start turning yellow, and with time the wool grease will turn rancid and start to smell.

I wash wool in a bucket of lukewarm water with a small amount of unscented washing-up liquid or wool detergent. It's important not to squeeze the wool too much or it will felt together. Submerge the wool a few times and leave it to stand for at least half an hour. Then discard the water, refill the bucket with fresh lukewarm water, carefully turn the wool over in the bucket and leave it to stand again.

When the rinsed water comes out relatively clean, I am happy. When the last lot of water has been discarded I try to squeeze the remaining water out of the wool as best I can. Then I place the wool in a towel and twist it so that the towel soaks up the water as it is squeezed out. Finally, I spread the wet wool out over newspapers on the floor. If you have underfloor heating, you're lucky because it will dry in no time! If you have a wooden floor you'll have to try something else as the moisture will leave marks; perhaps a few stacked wire baskets would work?

You can also buy prepared wool that is ready to be spun; just search for 'rolag' on the internet.

Card the wool

When the wool is dry, it's time to prepare it for spinning by untangling it and removing any lumps. A common way to do this is by carding the wool. For this you need two tools called carders. I sit with one leg crossed over the other and place a carder on my lap with the handle pointing away from me. I place the wool on top of the teeth of the carder with the fibres going vertically, then I grip the carder's handle with my left hand. With my right hand, I take the other carder and start carding by placing it over the wool and pulling the top carder towards me. The bottom carder I keep supported against my knee. Repeat the movement: the right-hand carder is lifted and placed on top of the left-hand carder, and then you pull the right hand backwards.

Sit with one leg crossed over the other and place one carder on your lap while you card.

At first it's easy to be too heavy-handed, and you might slam the carders together and then try pulling them apart. That won't work. Instead, think of it as like stroking a cat: place one carder gently on top of the other and then pull them apart.

After a while you will notice that the wool has moved from the left-hand carder to the right. Then it's time to turn the carders over so that you hold them both in front of your body with both handles pointing downwards. Rub them against each other by holding the right carder's bottom edge against the left carder's top edge, then pull downwards with the right carder so that the carders' 'palms' rub against each other. [1, 2]

Now the wool will swap carders. Turn the carders so that the handles point the opposite ways, place one in your lap and card through the wool again. I usually card through the wool three times before I am happy. Then I hold the carders with both handles downwards and rub them against each other a few times, going up and down. Now a small roll is formed of the carded wool, known as a rolag. Remove the rolag from the carder and hold it up to the light. Can you see any lumps or knots? If so, remove them.

1

2

Spin yarn from wool

When I card I usually prepare many rolags in one session. It's important to keep them somewhere where they don't get squashed together; for example, in a basket or a paper bag.

If you don't have carders but still want to spin, you can 'tease' the wool. When you tease wool you separate the locks buy pulling them apart with your hands to make the wool fluffy.

Spinning on a spindle

A spindle is a very simple tool consisting of a shaft with an added weight. Sometimes it has a hook at one end through which the thread runs; my spindle has a carved groove instead.

To get started, I recommend that you secure a length of yarn around the spindle's shaft, then wrap it clockwise around the shaft up to the hook. Now, take a rolag and place it on your left arm, on top of the hand. Hold your left index and middle fingers together out straight (I call this the 'cigarette' grip) while the thumb, ring and little finger grip a small amount of the wool and the end of the yarn. [3]

These three fingers (thumb + ring finger + little finger) I call the 'upper lock': you will soon realise why. With the wool in the left hand you will have the right hand free. With this you spin the spindle by gripping the top of the shaft with your thumb and index finger and rolling the shaft between your fingers by pulling the index finger towards you quickly then letting go. The shaft will start spinning clockwise. [4] It can be nice to sit down while you do this, because after a while the spindle will start spinning the other way and you might want to be able to catch it between your thighs so that it stops.

When you have put the spindle in motion you let it go and pinch around the starting fibre with your right thumb and index finger just under the left hand's fingers. Pull down a small amount of wool below the upper lock. These will now form the 'lower lock'. [5]

Spin yarn from wool

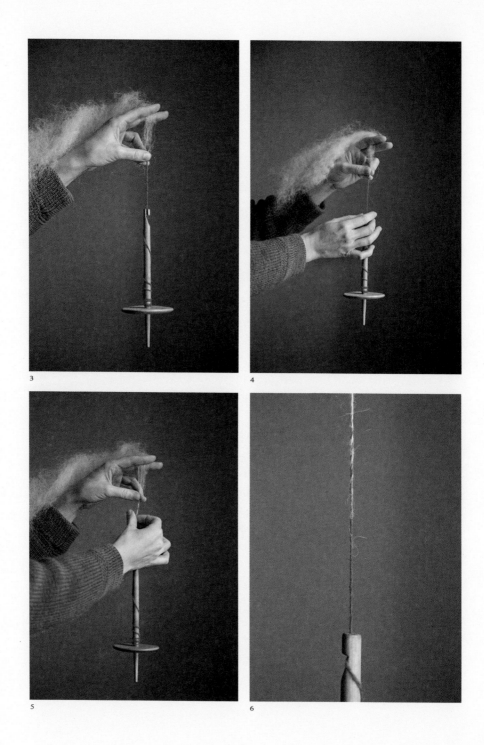

3

4

5

6

Spin yarn from wool

Between the upper and lower lock, you are in control

What turns the wool into a yarn is the twisting motion that is introduced when you make the spindle move. As the spindle spins, the yarn end it hangs to will spin too, and it will grip any wool fibres that it can catch. [6] If you don't limit the amount of fibre that the rotation gets access to, all the wool you have in your hand will form a lump that just gets bigger and bigger. You'll probably experience this when you start spinning. But that's okay; just spin the lump the other way and it will untwist.

This is where the finger locks come into the picture. When I spin, I put the spindle in motion, pinch the wool just under the upper lock (left hand) with the lower lock (right thumb + index finger) and pull a string of fibres that will become the new yarn. I pinch hard with my right hand's lower finger lock and don't let go until I am happy with the amount of fibre I have pulled down. Then I pinch with my left finger lock (the upper) and release the right-hand lock so that the spinning gets access to the fibres I just fed through. Since the upper lock is pinched the spinning won't get further than that and won't get access to the fibres that are on the rolag on top of my arm.

The rhythm of the spinning is:

- Pinch the upper lock.
- Put the spindle in motion with your right hand.
- Move the right hand up to the upper lock and pinch around the wool fibre. Now the right hand's fingers will form the lower lock.
- Pull the right hand downwards so that you feed through the fibres that are to be formed into yarn.
- Pinch the upper lock.
- Release the lower lock: The right hand will move downwards to spin the spindle again.

After a while, your yarn will be so long that the spindle will hit the floor. Then you unhook the yarn from the hook at the top of the spindle and wind it onto the spindle's shaft. Then you can continue spinning.

Spin yarn from wool

Troubleshooting

IF THE YARN BREAKS

Splice the yarn by fluffing up the wool in the broken-off end, place it in the upper finger lock together with a little bit of loose wool from the 'cloud' and continue spinning. The wool at the end of the thread will grip hold of the loose wool and you can simply continue.

IF THE YARN IS TWISTED TOO MUCH

For a beginner, a common occurrence is that the yarn twists too tightly and automatically starts to pull together to form little loops, then finally breaks off. This is due to spinning the spindle faster than you feed through the wool, so the relationship between the two gets off balance. Solve the problem by letting go of the yarn: leave it hanging to rotate as it wants and it will untwist itself. When you continue to spin you can practise spinning a longer thread before you spin the spindle again. Practise for a few hours and you'll soon get to grips with it.

Set the twist

When you have finished spinning you need to 'fix' the yarn before you start using it, or it will just start untwisting again when you try to make something with it. I think it works best to wind the yarn tightly onto something rigid and waterproof; for example, the lid of a lunch box, and then submerge the whole lid with yarn on it into warm water. Leave it for a while so that you know that the water has soaked into the yarn fully, then remove the lid and leave it to drip over a sink. When it has stopped dripping you can place it somewhere warm so that the yarn dries fully before you take the yarn off the lid. This way the yarn dries while taut and will become nice and even.

After a while your yarn will be so long that the spindle hits the floor.
Remove the yarn from the hook, wind it onto the spindle's
shaft and continue spinning.

Spin yarn from wool

Make thread from nettles

That linen fabric is made from the flax plant is common knowledge, but not everyone knows that the long stalks of nettles also contain fibres that can be spun! Nettle fibre is very similar to flax both in appearance and feel, and the finished thread won't sting you. Nettle fibre is slightly more fragile than flax fibre, but it's completely free and grows in abundance without you having to put in any effort, which are clear benefits.

YOU WILL NEED
- Gloves
- Wool carders or flower frog
- Saucepan
- Unserrated cooking knife
- A smooth surface to scrape the nettles against
- Spindle or spinning wheel

Find the right nettles

The fibres that can be made into textiles sit in the nettles' 'bark'; that is, the slightly fleshy layer around the harder stalk. The first step in making thread is to separate this outer layer from the stem.

In the places where 'branches' come out from the nettle's stalk there is a risk that the fibres will break. When you look for nettles to make into fibres you should therefore look for long stalks with as few branches as possible. My best place to find nettles is in a sparse birch forest with slightly damp ground, where they will grow long and straight!

Picking nettles in the summer

There are two periods in the year when it's good to pick nettles: late summer to early autumn, and mid-winter to late spring.

If you pick fresh nettles in late summer, you can pull off the leaves (which are not used in this project) and then pull off the green bark in long strips. Loosen the bark by placing the stalks on a smooth surface (tarmac works fine) and then step on them so you hear them crack. Divide the stalks in the middle along the stem. Thereafter you can easily remove the bark from the stalk.

While the strips of bark are fresh it's easy to scrape through to the fibres with an unserrated cooking knife by placing the strip against a smooth, but preferably slightly springy, surface: a worn-down shoe sole is perfect, but a chopping board will also work well. Soon light-coloured fibres will appear; the aim is to scrape off as much as possible of the green mass that surrounds them without breaking the fibres themselves. Save the light-coloured fibres and let them dry.

Picking nettles in the winter

If you pick nettles in the winter, the leaves and most of the stinging hairs have wilted away while the stalks remain, and look similar to dried grass.

If you have ever prepared flax you will remember that an important step in the process is to 'ret' the flax so the material surrounding the fibres breaks down. When you pick nettles in the winter, the retting

process has already happened in nature, so much of the preparation work is already done and the fibres are easy to extract. Look for nettles in shady spots; those that have been exposed to a lot of sun rarely have any good fibres left. Break the nettle in two and see if a band of bark and fibres comes loose. If it does, you can break the nettle apart piece by piece starting from the root end and pull the fibres off. There can be a big difference between nettles that have grown in the same spot; therefore I prefer to pick the nettles one by one and pull off the fibres directly instead of picking a large bunch and then pulling off the bark. If you're unlucky, half of the nettles you have picked might turn out unusable.

Make thread from nettles

Make thread from nettles

Soften up the fibres

When you have a handful of nettle bark, you can rub it between your palms. You can do this regardless of when you picked the nettles. Now the fibres are released. Continue until the bunch in your hands feels supple. If you picked nettles during winter, there will be a great deal of dust. Sit outside to work and wear a face mask. The dust is very fine and it's best not to inhale it.

Card the fibres

When the bark has turned into a bunch of soft fibres I take out a wool carder. If you don't have one you can use a flower frog, but beware of the spikes so you don't hurt yourself! Place the carder in your lap, place one end of the fibre bunch on top of the carder, place one of your palms over the fibres and pull the bunch from the carder. Fibres will get stuck in the carder, and when all the fibres are stuck you can take them out and start again. When you have carded through the fibres a few times you will have short fibres that are stuck on the carder and long fibres left in your hand. The long fibres you can set aside and the short ones you can lift off the carder.

Make thread from nettles

Wash the fibres

When you have combed through the fibres a few times you could spin them straight away, but I do the following to make them even softer and cleaner: bring water to the boil and add some grated soap flakes. I use about 1 tbsp flakes per litre (35fl oz) of water, but it's no exact science. Add the nettle fibres and leave them to soak overnight. Then rinse the fibres in lukewarm water and spread them out somewhere airy and leave to dry.

Card again and spin!

When the fibres have dried they will have become glued together, so I soften them up again by rolling them between my palms to be able to comb them through three or four times before I'm happy. Then I pick off the fibre 'cloud' from the carder, roll it together, and I'm ready to spin. You can follow the instructions on pages 103–105 (spin wool), but with one addition: keep a cup of water to hand and wet the thread as you spin by dipping your right hand's fingers in the water and running them over the newly formed thread. This will make the thread smoother and more compliant.

PS: If you have carded wool before you might want to pick up the second carder and card 'properly'. My experience is that it doesn't work very well for nettle fibres, as they break off easily and form little lumps.

Carving

My rule of thumb when I work with a sharp knife is that I should feel calm and safe. Carving towards yourself isn't dangerous by definition, but a grip where you don't have control is an unsafe grip even if someone else says it will be fine. Trust your own instinct, take it easy and take many short breaks. It's fun to carve, but it's when you get tired or unsure that you hurt yourself.

Another common cause for injury when working with a knife is that the knife isn't sharp. With a dull blade you need to use a lot more force and the knife is more likely to slip. I know it can feel scary to work with a super sharp knife, but for carving it's safer than a dull one.

I usually hold the knife fairly far down in my hand when I carve, so that a part of the blade is covered by my fingers, as in the picture. I hold my index finger bent over the blade's spine; this gives me better control over what I do with the knife than if I only hold the wooden handle. The grip will come naturally when you have carved for a while, but you can try straight away and see if you like it.

Carve a wall hook

Tree branches are built to carry a lot of weight, which makes them perfect to turn into wall hooks. Make sure to ask the landowner before you start sawing down trees or branches. If you find piled-up branches that have already been sawed off, however, it's usually okay to take what you want.

YOU WILL NEED
- Carving knife
- Saw
- Carving axe (optional)
- A young tree or branch with smaller branches on it
- Screwdriver and screws for hanging

Choose your branch

Making a hook from a natural branch doesn't have to be more complex than fixing it to the wall, but it's fun to make it a bit fancier. I made mine from a maple tree I cut into pieces with good branches on them. The thinnest branch was around 1cm (⅜in) thick. If the branches are thinner than that, they might not be very strong and won't make good hooks.

Carve a wall hook

Make the hook's flat back

If you want, you can axe, carve or saw off the back of the branch so that the hook sits flat against the wall. I chopped off a bit of material with the axe, then placed the branch on a level work surface to check if it lay flat or not. It didn't on the first try, but then I removed a little bit more, tried again and kept going until the hook could lie flat against the work surface.

Peel off the bark

It's often easy to peel off the bark from green wood, but don't use your best carving knife if the branch has been lying on the ground and become muddy. Little grains of sand in the mud can damage the edge of the knife. If you have both a freshly sharpened and a less precious carving knife in the toolbox, use the latter to peel the bark.

Cutting nice surfaces on curved wood

I had the idea that I would peel off the bark and then the wood underneath would shine golden, but when the tree's sap had oxidised, the surface wasn't as nice as I had hoped. Time to take out the carving knife again! Choose a sharp knife this time. Carving the outer layer of wood from a stick can be cosy and meditative – and super hard, when you come to the branch. Where the branch meets the stem, the wood's fibres go in all possible directions, and it's easy to end up with a lot of ugly cuts when trying to carve a nice surface there. But don't give up. Here I supported the work against my chest – a common working position when working with long pieces of wood. To get good control over how the knife cuts, I like to use a grip where I hold the knife in my right hand and then place the left hand's fingers over it. When I carve, I squeeze with both hands, which gives me a lot of strength and control. Now it's easy to carve nicely and evenly around the base of the branch.

Before you hang the hook

When the wood is green it's easy to work with, but the hook needs to dry before you can fix it to the wall. This is because green wood releases moisture while it dries and will also shrink slightly in the process. The wood can also crack a little while it dries, although that won't affect the strength of the hook. If you want to avoid cracks you can wrap the hook in a tea towel or paper bag and leave it to dry like that. How long the hooks need to dry depends on how thick they are, but give them 2–3 weeks before you put them up on the wall and it should be fine.

PS: When you are ready to fix the hook to the wall it's good to drill a hole in it first, otherwise there's a chance the screw will split the wood.

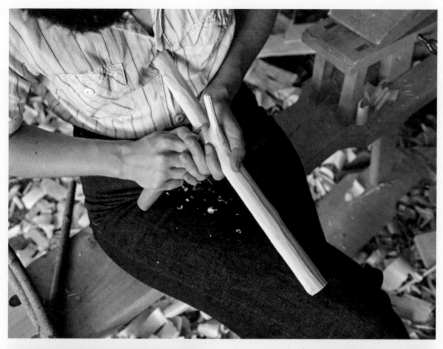

Carve a wall hook

Carve a peg rail

Peg rails can be made in many variations and look good in any room. Put one up in the hallway of a busy family home or, like me, make a rail with three pegs to hang your tea towels from.

YOU WILL NEED

- Drill with 9mm (3/8in) drill bit
- Carving knife
- Pencil
- Ruler or folding rule
- Saw
- Wood for the rail, at least 1.5cm (5/8in) thick
- Wood for the pegs, approx. 1.5 x 1.5cm (5/8 x 5/8in)
- Wood glue
- Linseed oil
- Paint
- Screws for assembly
- Baking paper to burnish the paint

Prepare a template

Start by making a template for how you want the pegs on your peg rail to look. I made mine in a fairly traditional form, but they don't have to look like that! I think it's nice if the pegs are wider than the tenon, but again, they don't have to be.

Choose your wood

I carved my pegs from square pieces of wood that I split away from a piece of dry birch wood. If you don't have a splitting knife and your own private wood stash you can go to a building-supply store and buy a square dowel. My pieces were about 1.5cm (⅝in) wide and 7.5cm (3in) long.

The rail to which the pegs are fixed I made from a 1.5 x 4.5 x 23cm (5/8 x 1¾ x 9in) piece of spruce wood.

Saw a 2-3mm (1/8in) deep notch all round at one end for the tenon and just across one side at the other end to mark the inside of the hook.

Saw out peg blanks

I started by sawing out blanks for my pegs. Then I drew a line with a pencil around the whole blank to mark where the tenon should start and a line for where the hook should be. Both lines ended up 1.5cm (⅝in) in from each short end, but at one end I drew on only one of the blank's four sides. At the other end I drew on all four sides.

Then I sawed a 2–3mm (⅛in) deep notch on all sides of the blank at the end with markings all the way around, and made the same cut on the one side that is marked at the other end of the blank. At the end that is sawed all the way around we will carve a tenon; at the other end, the single saw cut marks the beginning of the hook part of the peg.

Start carving

When I carve, I work with a series of different grips that almost all build on carving towards myself in a calm and controlled manner. I hold the knife in my right hand, hold my thumb against the wood for support, then make a squeezing motion so that the blade runs in the direction of my thumb. When I carve a peg like this the cut will stop automatically since I carve towards a sawed notch, but you won't always have that. If you have never carved before, try making the motion in the air a few times. Hold the knife and close the hand to a fist. The knife blade should land with the edge just to the right of your thumb and not straight onto the thumb, because then there is a big chance that you will cut yourself. The stages of carving a peg are shown in the photo on page 128.

I started by carving two diagonal bevels from the tenon's sawed tracks through to the beginning of the hook. The cut is shallowest where it begins and deepest where it ends. [1] Carve off wood shavings until you have reached the depth of the sawed track. If you cut deeper than the sawed notch you will need to cut off the shavings by pressing the knife down, across the fibres. [2]

Then I carve the top flat down towards the hook, and I carve diagonal bevels to round the edges, see pegs D and E. I also carve diagonal bevels on the back of the peg, see pictures 3, 4 and peg F. I then round the hook's tip to get a nice shape, see peg H in picture 5.

Carve the tenon

When I am happy with the shape of the peg, it's time to carve the tenon. Here you have the sawed track to guide you. Draw a ring, around the same size as the hole where the tenon will go, at the end of the tenon. Then start carving off the material around the tenon using small, calm cuts that end by the sawed track. [6]

When you think that the tenon is getting small enough, you can drill a 9mm (⅜in) wide test hole into a piece of scrap wood, and test the tenon by

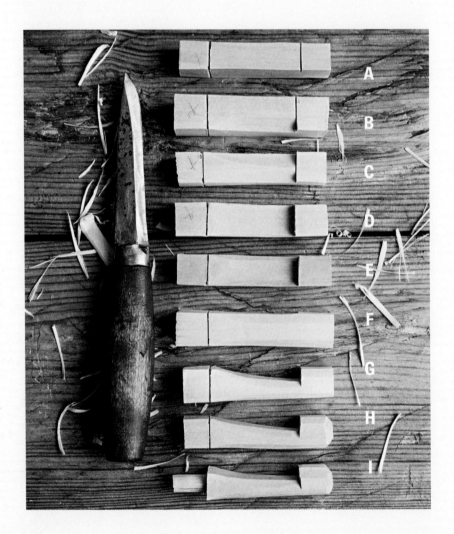

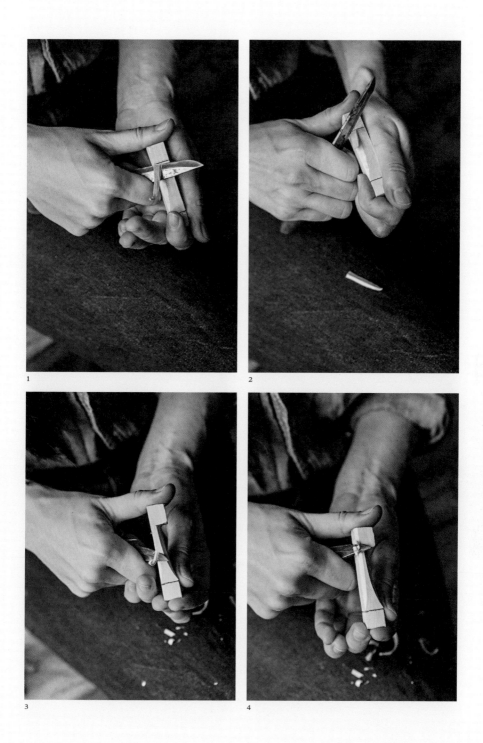

Carve a peg rail

5

6

trying to insert it into the hole. Carve off a little at a time from your tenon until you can push it down into the hole, but with as little margin as possible: the tenon should sit snugly. [7]

Prepare the rail

When all the pegs are finished it's time to work on the rail where they will sit. I carved off the outer surface of the wood with a carving knife, since I think it looks nice with a cut surface. But I should disclose that it can be a bit tricky to achieve a nice finish when carving with the type of cheap industrial wood that I used, which has a lot of branches and fibres going in all possible directions, so you easily end up with an uneven surface. If you think it's too tricky you can skip this step.

I painted my rail a light blue colour, then I added some detail by dipping an old toothbrush in white and black paint and pulling my finger over it, which I thought resulted in good-sized spatters. When the paint had dried I polished it by rubbing it with a piece of baking paper, which transformed the typical matt surface to a soft sheen.

7

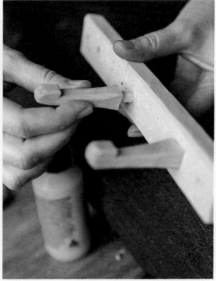
8

When the rail is finished you can mark out where the pegs should go and drill holes for the tenons, again using a 9mm (⅜in) drill bit. Add a small amount of wood glue to the inside of the holes, then push the pegs into place. [8] A tidy-minded person might think you should secure the peg with a small pin at the back, and you can certainly go ahead and do that. I think it's enough to glue the tenon in place provided that it fitted snugly from the beginning.

PS: Remember that there needs to be space for a screw that attaches the rail to the wall at each end of the rail, so don't place the pegs too far out at the edge. I think it looks nice if the screw sits around 2cm (¾in) in from each end of the rail. Pre-drill a hole in each end of the rail before you add the screw so that it doesn't crack.

Flaxseed pod hanging mobile

In Sweden we mainly grow oil-seed flax which produces flaxseed oil, but recently growing fibre flax has become more popular among hobby gardeners. At the top of the flax straw, the seed pod sits like a little golden globe. Since I love gathering beautiful things from nature, I thought about what I could do with these shining capsules. If you can't get hold of flaxseed pods perhaps try other dry seed cases or even flowers.

YOU WILL NEED
- Flexible twigs
- String 3 x 1m (39in)
- Flaxseed pods
- Needle and thread in a neutral colour such as brown or grey
- A keyring or other small metal ring

Make the rings for the base

The base of the mobile is made from two rings, one larger and one smaller, that are tied together with string. I made them from some twigs that I twisted into shape. Look for long, straight shoots that grow out of the ground – they are usually fine to bend. You can of course use ready-made metal rings instead.

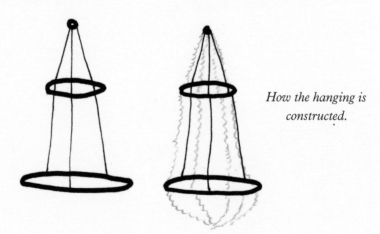

How the hanging is constructed.

Flaxseed pod hanging mobile

Assemble the base

When the rings are finished, hang the keyring up with a length of string and tie the three 1m (39in) lengths of string to it. Then tie the strings to the smaller ring, making sure that it is level – that is, tied to the same height on all strings. Tie with single knots to start off with, then it's easy to adjust the height of the ring until it is level. Then tie the larger ring a bit further down using the same strings – this should also be level. When you are happy with the placement of the rings you can cut the ends of the strings that are hanging down below the bottom ring and hide the ends on the bottom twig ring.

String up the seed pods

The seed pods are strung onto the sewing thread with the help of a needle. Measure your base to see how long the strings should be from the keyring down to the bottom ring and then in towards the middle point underneath it. Add around 20cm (8in) so you have a bit of extra length in case you need it. I think a minimum of six strings of seed capsules are needed to make a nice mobile, but it will look even better if you use more.

Flaxseed pod hanging mobile

Attach the strings of seed pods

Start attaching the strings by tying them to the keyring. Place them so you have the same number of seed pods between each section and evenly spaced. Take your sewing thread and start wrapping it around the top ring. When you come to the first string of seed pods, lift it up to give it a little bit of slack, then secure it in place by wrapping the sewing thread around it and the ring a few times. [1]

Secure the strings of seed pods to the bottom ring in the same way. They are not what hold the rings together, but should rather be draped over them. When the strings of pods have a bit of slack, the mobile will have a relaxed and elegant look.

Finally I bring all the strings together underneath the mobile, shorten them so that they're all the same length and tie them together so that I get a rounded shape at the bottom. [2]

When I have finished the mobile, I hang something underneath it to finish it off. I finished this mobile with a Japanese one-yen coin, which is said to bring good luck and shines nicely in the sun!

1

2

Flaxseed pod hanging mobile

Make a festive crown

Simple elegance has its place, but sometimes you need a flashy crown to brighten up the mood. This piece is inspired by the traditional headwear called *'lad'* that is a part of the folk costume of Malung. Such crowns are worn by brides for weddings, but my crown can be worn by anyone, anytime. The crown consists of a base made of corrugated cardboard that I have bent into shape, dressed in fabric and then decorated. Two tie bands at the neck keep it in place.

YOU WILL NEED
- A piece of corrugated cardboard approx. 50 x 20cm (19½ x 8in)
- Pen
- Scissors
- Ruler
- Fabric to cover the crown with
- Glue gun and glue
- Wood shavings or dried leaves
- Coloured drinks cans
- Beads
- A nail
- Hammer

Make a festive crown

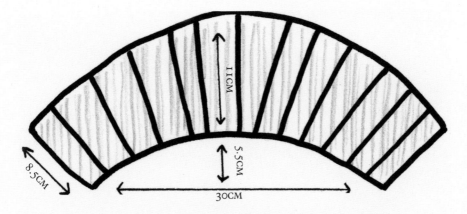

The blue lines mark the grooves in the cardboard, while the black lines show where the folds should go to get a round shape for your crown. For imperial units 8.5cm = 3⅜in, 11cm = 4 ⅜in, 5.5cm = 2⅛in, and 30cm = 12in.

Make a base

Start by drawing out the shape of the crown on the cardboard and cut it out. Take out the fabric you want to cover the crown with and use the cardboard as a template for cutting out two fabric pieces that are approximately 2cm (¾in) larger than the template on all sides.

Now start shaping the cardboard base by folding it according to the markings on the template.

I used a ruler that I bent the cardboard around to control the folds, which otherwise like to follow the corrugated cardboard structure. I placed the crown-to-be on my head to check the shape and folded and bent it until it had a rounded shape that sat well on my head.

Cover the base in fabric

Now cover the front of the base with one of the fabric pieces. Place the folded cardboard piece on a table and straighten out the fabric over it. Let it stand up; don't press it flat against the table as it will lose its shape. I straightened the fabric with my hands over the base and the edges of the fabric protruded fairly evenly around its edges. Then I took out the glue gun and secured the fabric by alternately gluing at the

 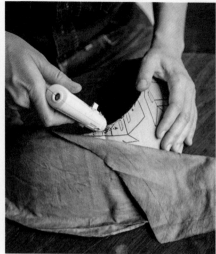

top and the bottom of the crown so I could stretch out the fabric while I glued to make sure it got completely straight. The fabric was folded and glued to the back, and here it can be tricky: along the bottom of the crown it will become difficult to fold the fabric around the edge. Make a few cuts along the edge of the fabric and it will be easier.

You might think it's unnecessary to cover the crown in fabric when it should be covered in wood shavings anyway, but I didn't want to risk any cardboard being visible in between the shavings, as it would ruin the festive feel.

Decorate the crown

I knew I wanted to make flowers from drink cans for my crown, but I needed something beautiful to fill out the rest of the surface. On my workshop floor there were some extra nice wood shavings that got the honour. I glued the shavings on overlapping so that they covered the whole surface of the crown. I started to glue a row along the top edge and then worked my way down. If you don't have wood shavings at home you can use something else. Dry, flat leaves I think would look great!

Make some metal flowers

Gather together different aluminium drink cans in colours that you like. Cut off the bottom and the lid (using scissors you're not too precious about) so that you get a flat metal sheet. Wash the metal sheet clean and bend it so that it lies flat.

Cut out two paper templates in the shapes of a larger and a smaller flower. Draw the flower shapes on the metal with a biro and then cut them out. I folded the petals one by one with my thumbnail to give the flowers shape, then I punched a hole in the middle of each flower using a hammer and a nail. Make sure you hammer onto a non-delicate surface so you don't get marks on your table; a chopping board works fine.

Assemble several flowers

I attached a small flower inside a larger one by running a threaded needle through both, then adding three glass beads to the needle and turning back again through the same hole. On the back of the flower, I secured the threads by tying the ends onto a small bead. I attached the flowers to the crown using a glue gun and complemented them with small golden leaves cut out of a caviar tube.

Make a festive crown

Add the ties

When I had finished decorating the front I glued two ties to the back of the crown, one to each bottom corner. I made the ties from the same fabric in which I covered the crown by cutting two long strips that I hemmed. You could use ready-made ties or ribbons as well.

Cover the back of the crown with fabric

Finally I covered the back of the crown with fabric by placing it flat against the cardboard, adding a string of glue approximately 5cm (2in) from the edge of the base between the cardboard and the fabric, then pressing together the fabric and the glue. The aim with this step is to get the fabric flat against the inside of the base, while the last 5cm (2in) towards the edges are loose. The next step is to fold in the edges of the fabric, so that the folds sit evenly with the edge of the crown, then glue them down so that no raw or frayed fabric edges are visible.

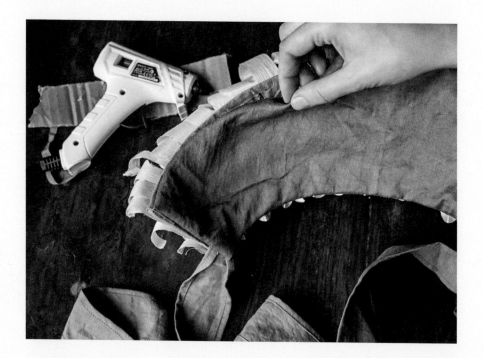

Afterword

Sometimes I think about handicrafts as a kaleidoscope. You add pretty much the same pieces, shake them up – and a whole new picture appears! Or object, in this case. There are so many possibilities in a piece of wood, a length of fabric or an old beer can, that it sometimes makes me dizzy. I'm sure you can combine many ideas from the book's different projects and come up with completely new things! A hanging mobile with beer-can flowers? A crocheted hat made from hand-spun yarn? You've got this: if you have got through this far you probably think handicrafts are rather fun. Here are a few tips to help you on your way.

Can I do it myself?

Do you think my instructions don't make sense? Perhaps you can see a cleverer way to solve a problem than I have? That's completely fine! Try it your way. Perhaps it's better, and perhaps you'll understand why I did it the way I did.

Ugly materials won't usually make an attractive item

Work with materials that you like. If the fabric isn't nice to start off with the chance that you will like the cap when it's finished is quite small.

Make multiples

Sometimes the secret to making nice things is that it's not enough to make one: you have to make multiples for it to seem impressive. The human eye loves repetition, and seeing multiples of the same object triggers some sort of ancient gatherer gene inside us. Sometimes I have made objects that I didn't think turned out that well, but when I made ten, all of a sudden they looked great! Besides, you will get a bit more skilful every time you repeat a craft technique.

Glossary

BLANK A piece of wood that has been prepared for further processing; for example, by removing the bark or cutting it to a certain length.

CARD To detangle and fluff up wool before spinning using a pair of tools called carders.

CARDERS Wooden tools that look like paddles and come in pairs. On one side the carder is covered in rubber or leather to which many metal teeth are attached.

CROWN (on a hat) The bowl-shaped part of the hat or the cap that covers the head.

DUPLICATE STITCH An embroidery stitch that looks like a knitted stitch.

EDGE The sharp part of a knife.

FULLED (fabric) A wool fabric that has been felted together to become dense with help from water and heat. On a fulled fabric it can be difficult to distinguish the individual threads in the weave.

FUSIBLE INTERLINING A fabric that is primed with glue that you iron on to apply. Used to reinforce other fabrics and make them sturdier.

GRAIN LINE You could describe this as 'In the same direction in which the thread runs in fabric'. In woven fabrics there are two thread directions, the warp and the weft, and they run at a 90-degree angle to each other.

GREEN WOOD Wood that has been freshly cut is still moist and is often called 'green'.

HANK (yarn) When the yarn is arranged in a series of long loops instead of being wound onto a bobbin or into a ball.

HEM To hem fabric means to fold it double and sew it down with a seam. You do this to conceal the raw edge that you get when cutting the fabric.

MORDANT Treating a yarn or fabric before dyeing it with a mordant makes the textile more receptive to dyes.

RET, RETTING To break down plant material with the help from a controlled decomposing process to the point where the remaining fibres become accessible for further processing into thread/yarn.

RIGHT SIDE (fabric) The front of the fabric; the side you want to be visible.

ROLAG A bunch of fibres that are formed when carding wool.

RUNNING STITCH Standard up and down stitches.

SEAM ALLOWANCE If you sew two pieces of fabric together with a seam that sits right at the edge of the fabric, the seam will come apart with the slightest pull. Therefore, you always cut the fabric panels slightly larger than they need to be when sewn together and sew a bit in from the edge. This is called the seam allowance.

SHAFT (spinning) A smooth stick that together with a whorl or weight forms a spindle.

SHANK A short shaft of thread on which a button sits. The shank's function is to form a gap between the button and the fabric and it is used when the fabric that is to be buttoned is thick.

SPINDLE A tool for spinning textile fibres; not to be confused with spinning wheel.

SPLITTING WOOD Splitting a piece of wood in two parts by beating a wedge-shaped object into it, for example an axe or a splitting knife.

STEM STITCH An embroidery stitch that forms a line, often used for depicting stems.
STITCH/STITCHES (knitting) The word is used to define the loops of yarn that form a knitted fabric.

STITCHES (crochet) The word is used to define the loops of yarn that form a crocheted fabric. Double crochet (US single crochet) stitches are worked into a previous row of stitches, while chain stitches are crocheted like a free-hanging chain.

STRAIGHT WHIP STITCH A stitch used to keep edges in place. The stitch is characterized by small, straight stitches at the front of the work and diagonal stitches at the back of the work.

TEASE To pull the fibres in a lock of wool apart with your fingers to untangle them and make them easier to spin.

TENON The part of the peg that is inserted into a rail.

THROAT PLATE A small plate that sits under the sewing machine needle, with a hole which the needle passes down through to the bobbin case.

TOPSTITCH (sewing) A line of stitching that is used to keep layers of fabric in place and reinforce a garment.

TWILL LINE The pattern of diagonal lines that is typical in denim fabric.

UPPER LOCK and **LOWER LOCK** These are not established terms in spinning; they are terms I have invented to explain what to do with your fingers while spinning.

WRONG SIDE (fabric) The back of the fabric; the side you don't want to be visible.

YARN OVER (crochet) To place the yarn around the crochet hook, so that you can then hook onto it with the tip of the crochet hook and pull it through one or several stitches that sit around the crochet hook's shaft.

First published in the United Kingdom
in 2025 by
Batsford
43 Great Ormond Street
London
WC1N 3HZ

An imprint of B. T. Batsford Holdings Limited

ISBN 9781849949569

A CIP catalogue record for this book is available from
the British Library.

10 9 8 7 6 5 4 3 2 1

Reproduction by Rival Colour Ltd, UK
Printed by Dream Colour, China

This book can be ordered direct from the publisher at
www.batsfordbooks.com, or try your local bookshop.